Universal Basic Income and the Threat to Democracy as We Know It

Universal Basic Income and the Threat to Democracy as We Know It

Peter Nelson

BEP BUSINESS EXPERT PRESS

Universal Basic Income and the Threat to Democracy as We Know It

First published in 2018 by
Business Expert Press, LLC
222 East 46th Street, New York, NY 10017
www.businessexpertpress.com

ISBN-13: 978-1-94819-864-6 (paperback)
ISBN-13: 978-1-94819-865-3 (e-book)

Business Expert Press Economics Collection

Collection ISSN: 2163-761X (print)
Collection ISSN: 2163-7628 (electronic)

Cover and interior design by Exeter Premedia Services Private Ltd., Chennai, India

First edition: 2018

10 9 8 7 6 5 4 3 2 1

Printed in the United States of America.

Abstract

Some of the greatest minds of the century have predicted that, up to at least 80 percent, if not more, of the world's workforce will be replaced by computers or artificial intelligence, the only uncertainty is about the time frame. The average prediction on timing of losses appears to be about 30 years, but many believe it will be sooner. No matter the exact period, the impact on our planet will eventually be enormous because governments will still need to find a way to provide the unemployed with money on which to live and a Universal Basic Income, a UBI, or something like it, is proposed to be paid to everyone without means test. That solution might appear well in theory, but the large numbers of unemployed will not want to be marginalized and will demand over time that the UBI be increased. Following human nature, under a democratic system as we know it, supposedly based on one person one vote, people will vote for whoever gives them more, and more, until the economic system breaks down unable to afford the payments. The question is whether democracy will survive the challenge or whether we finish with a benign group of bureaucrats at the top who decide what is in the best interests of the majority and the rest of the global population just accept it.

Keywords

employment, occupational choice, skill demand, technological change, universal basic income, wage inequality

Contents

CHAPTER 1

Introduction

Some of the greatest minds of the century have predicted that up to at least 80 percent, if not more, of the world's workforce will be replaced by computers, robots, or artificial intelligence lumped together as AI, the only uncertainty being the time frame. The average prediction appears to be about 30 years for most jobs to be replaced, but many believe it will be sooner. This covers with a broad and daily expanding brush, the way new technology is replacing jobs as are currently defined and looks at the period over which this will likely occur. It looks at what AI might contribute toward formulation of new jobs even in the face of the changing climate. The focus is not so much about listing which jobs are on the way out, but providing an illustration that suggest that most of them are, while at the same time, pointing out that any new AI-based jobs are unlikely to replace what is lost. The analysis is more on trying to draw attention to the problem of how this will impact democracy and to bring focus on its importance, where to date, no government appears to have taken the long-term probability seriously.

No matter the exact period of total job losses, the impact on our planet will be enormous because governments will still need to find a way to provide the unemployed with money on which to live and a Universal Basic Income, a UBI or something like it, is proposed to be paid to everyone without means test. Models of UBI have been instigated on a limited scale, but no one has looked at an overall impact on government structure.

The study of the future requires analysis of the benefits of a UBI along with its shortcomings, and because the subject deals with humans and humanity, it looks at the role which gender might ultimately play in elimination of jobs and the eventual possible world domination by either women or computers. Along with those possibilities is the need to look at what will have to change as jobs disappear and if a UBI or overall flat-line social welfare system is to be introduced can this be funded and on what legal framework.

Hypothesizing that a UBI is eventually introduced, this raises important issues not only regarding what people do with 100 percent leisure time, which might appear attractive in theory, but with low levels of payment, that high percentage of unemployed will not want to be marginalized and will demand over time that their UBI be increased.

The likely stages of introduction will be important to individuals in a specific country, but facing a global economy, geopolitical structures will see a rollout of the system across the globe. As history has demonstrated, large disaffected numbers of a society can rebel against the established order and military intervention is always a possibility.

As human nature will have it, under a democratic system, supposedly based on one person one vote, people will vote for whoever gives them more, and more, until the economic system would break down unable to afford the UBI payments. The question is whether democracy will survive the challenge or whether the world finishes with a benign group of bureaucrats at the top of a global government who decide what is in the best interests of the majority and the rest of the population must just accept the consequences.

If this is not a world people want, and democracies are to survive, planning for the eventualities outlined need to be considered seriously at individual and global government level. Logic suggests there being a trigger point in job loss numbers from which a UBI will be introduced, after which it will be too late to turn back and democracy as it is currently recognized will be finished.

CHAPTER 2

The Future of Employment

According to most of the great minds of the century, including Stephen Hawking, Elon Musk, Google's Chief Ray Kurzweil, or as outlined in the recent study of the McKinsey Global Institute,[1] robotics or artificial intelligence (AI) in one form or another will replace most jobs.[2] Hawking predicts machines will have replaced humans in 100 years. According to a survey of a broad section of AI experts, AI will probably take over most jobs in the next 50 years.[3] The World Bank estimates 57 percent of jobs could be automated within the next 20 years. There seems to be little dispute about the event, only differences of opinion on the timeframe. The question then becomes, what is to be done about it? No one seems to know how to move forward because of so many unknown factors.[4] Even if they do, no one has yet looked seriously at how this will affect the politics of the world as understood today.

The question of job losses is nothing new. John Maynard Keynes predicted widespread technological unemployment "due to our discovery of means of economising the use of labour outrunning the pace at which we can find new uses for labour."[5] This was an extension on governments having to pay people to dig holes and then filling them in again. This system only works while governments still can generate enough money from other sources to be able to pay the ditch diggers. Unfortunately, there is a tendency to create money by printing more of it when the supply runs out, creating a further problem because its purchasing power is reduced.

---

[1] MGI, *What the future of work will mean for jobs, skills, and wages*, November 2017.

[2] BBC interview. Released in open letter made public on January 12, 2014.

[3] *All hail our robot overlords*; Mike McRae.

[4] McKinsey MGI Report op.cit.

[5] John Maynard Keynes, The Economic Possibilities of Our Grandchildren (1930) in Essays in Persuasion, 1933.

Future predicted losses in the work force occur on a daily basis as reported in the press and on various websites. Starting the new year of 2018, Futurism's Claudia Geib[6] featured the hype of what the future would bring viewed from 100 years back. Many of the predictions from that time have been realized in one form or another, even when the technology that would bring in the ultimate invention had yet to be conceived. This as with predictions for TV type images which could be projected at home through telephone connections, well before TV had been invented. A common feature in projections was that new technology would reduce the need for workers, not increase their numbers.

From a recent Oxford and Yale University study, surveying 1,600 academics, the researchers were able to put likely timeframes on jobs that will be replaced, from, as an example, truck drivers gone within six years and off the road completely in 20. This study established a base line for repetitive job loss and for those that still require human to AI interface, such as where drivers are still required by law to be present in driverless vehicles. On an advanced level were predictions of AI's ability to write a best seller for the *New York Times* best seller list within 26 years and a top pop song written by a machine in 12 years. More worrying for humanity has been the prediction that, within 50 years, AI will be developing itself and then replacing humans in 80 years, or in Hawking's estimates, not even requiring humans in 100 years.

Where the period is the main issue in dispute, even with current guesses, care needs to be taken that the predictions might just be conservative when looking for example at how quickly *Uber* caught everyone, especially the taxi industry by surprise. Driven by an app, with Uber, there is almost no human interface and the next step is to replace even the driver.

The experts predicted in 2015 that AI machines would not be sufficiently advanced to beat the world *Go*[7] champion, *Ke Jie,* and yet, this

---

[6] Gloria Geib, www.Futureism.com "Does life in 2018 live up to what we predicted 100 years ago?", January 4, 2018.

[7] Abstract strategy board game for two players, aiming to surround more territory than the opponent.

was accomplished by a robot in 2017.[8] In a new paper, Google researchers detail how their latest AI evolution, *AlphaZero*, developed *superhuman performance* in chess, after being programmed with the rules it took just four hours to learn. It then obliterated the world champion chess program, *Stockfish*,[9] which had already defeated humans.

What can be seen is that AI will initially replace some jobs completely. Others will be partially replaced, and in the first instance, AI will simply assist in supporting various professions. Quoted have been examples of databases allowing paralegals to download every reference to any law on a legal question and then to further refine these to specifics for a particular case.[10] In medicine, there will be increased ability for individuals to self-diagnose and to identify their own treatment. Even now doctors are Googling symptoms during consultations along with searches for appropriate medicines which might be available for treatment. Take that one step further and *Xiaoyi*, an AI-powered robot in China, has recently taken the national medical licensing examination and passed with a score of 456 points, which is 96 points above the required marks to be registered as a doctor.[11] This robot, developed by leading Chinese AI company *iFlytek*, had been designed to capture and analyze patient information and then draw appropriate conclusions. They have proven that *Xiaoy*i could also have enough medical knowledge to be a licensed practitioner.

These examples are simply about someone programming all known knowledge into a system and then designing the selective program on the data to achieve a designated result.

The advances in technological application will have positives as well as negatives effects. As the taxi industry fought Uber, doctors are already insisting that governments legislate for doctors' prescriptions to be required for most common drugs in a fight against self-service medicine. While people might currently be forced to pay to go to a doctor for a prescription, it will not be long before the same patients realize that it

---

[8] Google's AlphaGo wins, but in 1997, *New York Times* article Reddit's futurology thread Yull-Ban predicted this could not be done before 2100.

[9] Peter Dockrill, Science Alert, December 7, 2017.

[10] Australian Broadcasting Commission, *The AI Race*, October 21, 2017.

[11] *Chinadaily*, *ZME Science*, https://futurism.com/?p=111790&post_type=post

is possible to buy just about anything online. For now, there remains a certain placebo effect and reassurance in seeing a physical doctor, but this will not always need to be the case and GP doctors' jobs will be gone.

Then again, if the first level of approach in medicine replaces GPs, while computer-simulated body anatomy is available for doctors to understand how it works, where do surgeons get the feel of live tissue with no more dissecting rooms? Obviously onscreen graphics can help teach, but there is a difference in seeing and interacting with a body in real life.

Low on the list of job replacements will be judges where some human interface is required although this is challenged by the University of Maryland's trailing of a Deception Analysis Reasoning Engine (DARE) on courtroom trial videos designed to show whether people are lying or not. While polygraphs are for now not permitted in American courts, the new system is aiming for a high degree of accuracy with facial recognition where it is likely to be accepted. If computers provide details of all appropriate laws and evidence can be certified as true, subjective analysis is reduced and even judges could be eliminated. At least, AI could reduce the need for the number of judges.

Questioning the demise of politicians could be difficult and will depend on what political system might evolve long term. Politicians will not like a DARE system that could indicate when someone is lying, and there will always be subjective issues around how the political machine and elections are conducted.

Constraints against future progress will continue, where wealthy vested interests will ensure that legislation will not interfere with their cash flow. The Western Australian revolutionary invention of a rotary *Wankel* engine completely changed the concept of piston driven motors, yet this would have seriously affected the established global auto industry, and so the technology was purchased and never reached the market.

The question of whether labor unions will have any significant role in reversing the job loss surge appears answerable in the negative. The power of the unions has been receding because fewer people had jobs for life. Technology has changed, and in part, unions have damaged themselves by some of the deals done with corporations against the interests of their members[12] and striking does not help retain jobs. Tracking irregularities was far more difficult in the past. The point here being that unions are unlikely to save the day in job retention.

A major concern on replacing workers will be its geographical effect. Individuals in wealthy countries may believe they can fight some type of rear guard action until money runs out, but less developed countries could be seriously impacted. While there remain pay differentials and job opportunities between countries, there will always be pressure on movement between markets. This can have serious consequences if something goes wrong in one country.

Early predictions have suggested that developing countries will be the hardest hit with extremes in overall job loses, such as Ethiopia losing 88 percent of jobs in the near future, Nepal 80 percent, and even China 77 percent.[13] The theory is that countries with large-scale low-paid workers focused on manual work will be hardest hit. Again, the unknown remains the timeframe.

Looking at the effect of major losses in one country, take as an example the textile industry in Bangladesh employing well over four million workers, in over 5,000 factories, 90 percent being women.[14] As the third largest garment exporter in the world, earnings bring in around 25 billion U.S. dollars annually. Nike already make their shoes by robot, and one could argue that, as clothing can easily be made by automatic machines, the only reason Bangladesh still employs its workers is because, with so many scattered factories and low pay, the financial return on machines is not yet worthwhile. With many small factories, it is also not easy to bring legal action against sweat shops nor attach stigma to a well-known brand. Close one factory and they can morph quickly somewhere else. This is more about marketing, transport, and customs duties than production costs because an identical shirt purchased in Bangladesh for three

---

[12] Australian famous case of Australian workers' union negotiating deal with employer for better terms against lower worker wages.

[13] Luke Kingma, Futurism, *https://futurism.com/images/universal-basic-income-answer-automation/*

[14] *http://worldometers.info/world-population/bangladesh-population/*

dollars is sold in Australia for 45 dollars.[15] The move to mechanization can change. What happens if four million people out of 165 million (3 percent) suddenly become unemployed? Should mechanization take place, it would also be a rapid introduction as soon as the savings become clear. Once one machine proves the economies of scale, others must follow immediately to remain competitive. Similar change could happen overnight in the garment industry worldwide. This might appease Western consciousness over not exploiting poorly paid workers with sweat shops closed, but will probably not be appreciated by the people losing their jobs. Bangladesh is just an example to bring home the possible effect on one developing (and poor) country, but this could be multiplied in countries all over the world.

There are also, as an example, millions of poorly paid outsourced data-entry people in India and the Philippines who could be replaced overnight as soon as even their tasks are automated as recordings replace human telephone answering.

The final part of the problem mix becomes the loss of jobs at the same time as populations expand, where to exacerbate the problem, the poorer countries still have the highest birth rates. Consequently, overall, the prognosis for job retention does not appear good, but the consideration here is not about a full analysis of what jobs might be lost, only in pointing out that this seems inevitable. The focus is directed to the potential political effect of large job losses, while asking what can and should be done in response.

---

[15] Author's personal review in Bangladesh and Australia.

CHAPTER 3

Progression of Disappearing Jobs

Consensus suggests that many manual repetitive jobs will go first. Again, link these to the less educated and the poor. Then, the progression is for the human applications to be taken over requiring higher intelligence and then to the super intelligent levels where computers can do most of the work better than humans and can even program themselves. Here, the time frame is again complicated to predict. In the "Go" championship example, the computer first made mistakes and then reprogrammed itself with the options it missed to enhance the defense. In the chess championship example, every recorded chess game was fed into the computer, so it could choose and adjust its responses. *Singularity* is the term used where the computers improve themselves and their functionality without human intervention, the end point being where the computers replace their makers or programmers. This has been covered in poignant science fiction for ages.[1] The question is how quickly AI will get to the stage where it can self-program more basic functions. In part, they seem to be able to do this already on the more sophisticated applications, but this is not perhaps warranted in automatic vacuum cleaners.

An Oxford study reported on the BBC regarding potential job losses identified nine skills people needed and used to survive replacement, including "social perceptiveness, negotiation, persuasion, assisting and caring for others, using originality, fine arts, and requiring finger and manual dexterity." Consequently, the careers most immune to automation required employees to negotiate, help, and assist others, and come up with creative ideas. The jobs utilizing these skills least likely to be

---

[1] In the movie 2001: *A Space Odyssey*, dealing with HAL (**H**euristically pro-grammed **Al**gorithmic) computer.

automated included social workers, nurses, therapists, and jobs that required creative and original ideas, as with artists and engineers, perhaps even women's hairdressers. There is no machine yet that can sheer sheep, so sheep shearers would think they are safe, yet someone has invented a drug that will make the wool fall off. Consequently, it would appear that few jobs are immune.

It is not intended to venture deeply into AI within the sex industry, but it is involved. A company, Realbotix, has designed interactive robot dolls that can speak and respond to emotions and stimulus. Looking human and with skin texture like a person, they can also provide verbal responses. For some reason, their prototype language chosen for the figure as most appealing was Scottish. The point here is to demonstrate how close to humans the robots have really come[2] and point in the direction of further possibilities no matter how extreme.

In January 2018, China announced in the world press that 20 percent of its munitions factories are now run by robots, presumably to remove danger experienced from past accidents. Whole factories now assemble vehicles. The list of possibilities for robot superiority goes from its already-folding laundry (in 2017 predicted to take another five years), writing high-school essays in eight, a retail salesperson going before 15, a surgeon within 25 years, and then automation of all human jobs in 80 to 100 years. Many people make predictions, yet no one can be sure.

Otherwise, accounting, insurance, and financial planning have all given way to computers as have audit systems, first outsourced and then computerized. In accounting, sophisticated programs accept data entry and cater for legal requirements while providing add-on programs for financial management. In relation to outsourcing, as an example, an Australian registered audit company of self-managed super funds[3] has this compliance program set up on a computer, cheap labor in India adds the data into the program and sends it back for the registrar's signature and for filing with government. Only that one signing is legally required satisfying compliance and no way can local human wages compete. Legislators

---

[2] In 2017, Saudi Arabia granted citizenship to a robot named Sophia.

[3] Evolve Pty Ltd., Australia.

have not felt inclined to curtail this outsourcing, but it would be possible to tax the outsourcing system itself.

Similarly, standard company audits are run through computer systems that go through far more checks that the sampling of the past and a qualified single person, then signs off on the results. The rest is covered by their liability insurance, made cheaper given the better reliance on AI than with human verification. Offices themselves have in many cases become *virtual*, shared, and used physically only when required for meetings, thereby doing away with many support staff.

Legal contracts now include almost every clause ever considered because it is simple to do and for a computer to print whole documents where previously lawyers had to select pertinent material only. Once data has been coded into a suitable storage bank, it becomes a simple matter to program for what is required. The quantum leap here is where every law firm does not have to have its own data bank, but one company can rent access to its storage, reducing the need for individual updates. Arriving at decisions from the database may work well when seeking a determination on case law, but in common law dealing with precedent, while programs could handle that, one could hope that some *humanity* might remain when handing down court decisions. The danger is that if an AI system cannot handle mitigating circumstances, (self-defense), a program might just ignore this all together.

In applying the AI to the legal side, it has become easier for governments to track tax avoidance schemes by accessing data through banks, financial institutions, and stock exchanges. The problem remains accessing the information in noted tax havens, but even the Swiss have agreed to supply account details to the U.S. tax authorities of Americans holding Swiss bank accounts.[4] The connected issue here in tracking down wealth of individuals held below the radar, while obviously necessary to curtail illegal activity, it discourages wealthy to make money on which they do pay tax. Governments understand this; so, on the one hand, they want to discourage these investors, while on the other side, they want to encourage them to use their money.

---

[4] This is only if there is a declaration that the account holder derives U.S. income.

When Hong Kong Chinese worried about the hand back to China and wanted a second option, many headed for Australia or Canada. The father sent the family off to establish a new home in Chatswood or Richmond where businesses were established with transfer pricing showing small profit in host country and the majority of profit made in HK where no tax is paid on export business. The point in this is that AI can provide means of tracing these tax avoidance schemes, but governments are, at the same time, reluctant to do this if it slows growth or reduces jobs.

Then, where film stars might believe they would not be replaced, there are increasing numbers of animated cartoons and the bringing back of old movies and actors such as Princess Lia from Star Wars 1977, reappearing in another episode during 2016. Movies can be reengineered and even Kevin Spacey on TV in *House of Cards,* cast as a U.S. President overnight disappeared from a hit series he was already filmed in, using technology to clone in a different person.[5] Take the music industry and most of the currently released songs have heavy production engineering and would sound nothing like the same song from a straight recording. One step further and take for example the five-track, heavy metal album just released, *Coditany of timeness*, produced by a computer. This was done by feeding an album called *Diotima by Krallice* into a neural network. Songs were broken down into short chunks and the system was asked to project how the next section of the new track would sound, a common methodology for teaching an artificial intelligence how to operate. Over three days, the track was produced after five million guesses at how a black metal song should sound.[6]

Where these estimates of jobs disappearing are important comes from their immediacy, because they will start taking effect in the current population's life time, and while all surgeons and doctors might not have to worry immediately, the timeframe must influence learning and practice. Few people will ultimately want to spend years studying for a profession that is on its way to being replaced by machines. Will a musician gain the same benefit from programming a computer to write the song than from

---

[5] Robin Wright replaces Kevin Spacey in currently filmed series and next eight episodes.

[6] Brad Jones, Databots, December 05, 2017.

playing it themselves? Schools and universities will need to change their emphasis, and already, computer teachers are entering the classrooms. Technology advancement is so rapid that it does not appear that current learning systems are designed to keep pace.

While it was early on argued that jobs requiring personal interface would still be required, there are now self-checkouts at supermarkets and McDonald's outlets, among others, have introduced increasingly more self-select consoles, reducing the need for counter staff. Japan has installed an extensive variety of machines offering a wide choice of food and drinks. There are now machines that dispense almost everything from films, books, clothing, tickets, and medical needs.

This self-service area also opens the question of banking that has, for some years now, replaced tellers with serve yourself options through ATMs, enhanced now with facilities on your smartphone where credit cards are no longer required. The next step as a logical extension is to have individual humans microchipped so that payments can be made by the wave of an arm instead of using their phone. Companies have already microchipped employees, so they can control opening doors and access security levels on computers through simple proximity. If they want the job, they need to get chipped. Add then how, instead of barcodes on supermarket products, the goods could also be *chipped*. The individual only needs to go to the store, select what they want, walk out and their own implant chip sends details of the purchases that are charged to the buyer's account.[7] Extending that and there are other smartphone options working through an implant with houses or apartments programmed to respond to an individual's arrival or departure. Add where everyone will have facial recognition systems doing the same, just as parking stations now work on photographs of your vehicle number plate, calculate the length of your stay and bill the driver on exit, all without physical contact.

Once everyone is chipped, instead of having a social security card of some kind, governments will be able to control people and also collect ongoing data on likes and dislikes, deciding what products a store should stock and presumably give data on voting preference. Would

---

[7] Author correspondence with IBM working on such a system.

voting if this should continue also be something organized automatically through an individual's chip? What happens to *fake news*? Will individuals be permitted to opt out from being chipped, and if not, is the penalty forced chipping?

While the list of advances due to AI appears endless, what it highlights is that nothing appears immune from technology, and it becomes a question of set up against labor cost. Entry and setup costs can be high, so a large store or chain can introduce such new technology into their operations, while the local corner store would not be able to afford the outlay and will close. More jobs lost. Amazon has expanded by running its operations on debt instead of share capital, with shareholders looking for their returns from share price increase, a system that gives them advantage over traditional corporations. As the AI advances with a move two steps forward, there is often one step back, where Amazon's retail launch into Australia in December 2017 was not all it hoped to be, and now, Amazon and Google are fighting over net neutrality. These appear to be minor setbacks, but a small business does not even have a voice. The big operators continue global expansion where Decathlon opening its first mega store in Australia announced that they were not worried by other stores knowing that they can be set to dominate the global sporting goods retail sector wiping out smaller competition.[8] The giants in various sectors could wipe out even big stores and their employees where perhaps only the biggest survive.

Amazon's financing methods have an unpleasant effect of being able to wipe out competition to then increase prices, but this demonstrates a whole new way of operating. The same extends to advertising, where regulators have sights set on Google, which has been reported as taking over 40 percent of the digital marketing in Australia in just four years, almost wiping out main stream media advertising revenue and the people this employs.[9]

Payments for different services are becoming increasingly computerized where there is now already difficulty in paying for many things in cash. The likely outcome will be that all services and bills will eventually

---

[8] Opened in Tempe, Sydney, December 2017.
[9] Steve Price, Macquarie Network, 2GB Money News, December 08, 2017.

be deducted automatically from bank accounts, and if overdrawn, the account is automatically debited with an interest charge. People replaced once more.

With the rise of cryptocurrencies, which could replace money as it now exists, Bitcoin being the current leader of these, it is possible to buy and sell between people prepared to accept these *currencies*. As with most new things, this cryptocurrency market is becoming flooded, and there will be many unhappy people during its development where just as one example, within one week, Bitcoin saw a 25 percent dive,[10] while *Independent Reserve*, a separate Australian cryptocurrency trader made a huge gain. On November 27, 2017, a Bitcoin hit 10,000 U.S. dollars, then 13,000 U.S. dollars a few days later. It then shot further upward and then down again. In Bitcoin, what it represents is an artificial product of which only 21 million *coins* are to be released. Hence, with restricted supply, people and now institutions are betting the price will go up. This cannot go on indefinitely, as ultimately someone will lose. The system works the same way as with a company registered with a set number of shares, which for public companies can be traded. However, companies make profits to influence prices, whereas with cryptocurrencies for now, there is simply limited supply and advertising to push up demand. With enough gullible buyers who do not understand the system, price can be driven up in the belief that everyone is making money. Governments are attempting to get in on the regulatory act and have concern that Bitcoin is an ideal product to use on the *Black* or *Dark Web,* used for illegal purposes and is a preferred method of exchange for drug dealers. It needs to be remembered that there is no security when dealing with Bitcoin, if hacked there is no recourse. There are, however, banks that will hold the bulk of a person's Bitcoin and owners only take out what they need. Bitcoin is now firmly in the government's eye, but many similar products could surface.

Responding to the current interest in the United States, the second largest bank, Bank of America, has just won a patent for a crypto exchange system, which they intend to develop for corporate clients. The system would theoretically be able to easily convert one digital currency

---

[10] This was on first week November 2017. Then, went to record 8,000 U.S. dollars on November 20, 2017.

into another while establishing the exchange rate between those two currencies based on external data.[11]

The current situation still leaves the system wide open for the regulators trying to establish systems for tracing the transactions in this *unofficial* currency market. It opens avenues in which wealth in some form or other could be put up in a *cloud* or on one of many *dark webs* and stay one step ahead of government's attempting to regulate or tax. The same applies to any artificial currency because legislation has trouble taxing change in value when not denominated in an official and traded currency. Legislators will eventually address this area and computers may aid the control transactions while, at the same time, allowing systems to stay one step ahead of the tax man. If someone owns a robot, or if robots have a legal status,[12] will it be possible for that robot to have a bank account and then who owns that account? Where is the robot domiciled? How about Bitcoin in Trust accounts? There remain so many great exciting questions.

Linked to the cryptocurrency development, there is now a conceptual *climate coin* version that is intended to allow everyone to participate in the fight against *climate change*. The idea is that the *coin* is rewarded when carbon outputs are reduced supposedly democratizing the carbon markets through blockchain technology. This is similar to systems allowing cash on increases or decreases of carbon emissions, but translated through a cryptocurrency, which could be used for other purposes. All of this development is relevant to job losses because increasingly financial transactions are transferred to AI interface and automated procedures. The overall face of banking can be seen to eventually move into a cloud.

Looking at how jobs disappear, and trying to determine what job is last to fall, how about in sport? There are already robot *boxing* matches or at least events where one robot attempts to destroy another. Will there be soccer, or rugby matches with two-sided robot opponents, and although this is quite possible, is it the same spectacle as when two teams of humans bash into each other? Do humans feel a twinge of empathetic pain when two machines smash each other as they do when two humans collide? If all moves are preprogrammed, will it be exciting to see rugby,

---

[11] www.Futurism.com December 07, 2017.

[12] See Saudi Arabia op.cit, granting *Sophia* citizenship in 2017.

as an example, becoming a robot contact-free sport? How about athletics where limits must be programmed or there is no end to what speeds runners might achieve? Another possibility would be physical games between robot versus human teams where robotic limits would need to be established or it would be obvious how that would finish. As robots take over, will robots start constituting part of the audience?

The list of possible sports for robot participation is extensive, and robots could be introduced into all of them even if originally they were to test human dominance.[13] The question is whether, as with the robot boxing matches, this becomes more of a contest between robot programmers than between the *athletes* themselves demonstrating one more win for AI and a loss for sportsmen. Will robotics in sport build recognition for *obese* programming athletes who have been overlooked in the past?

While there are jokes about robots, at the extremes of what robots might leave for humans, it is currently not possible to see a robot telling a joke except by repeating a joke from a data bank. This would be because it would need to analyze a situation requiring a joked response and then determine what response may or may not be appropriate? For a computer to make a subtle joke would require a database of all human knowledge and methods of benchmarking the algorithm's subtlety.[14] How does it tell the difference between a responsive, a good, or a bad joke? Could a robot understand an *Irish joke* or a *blond joke*, or know when it might be funny and to whom? How many jokes have a sexual connotation in which the sensitivity of the joke is important? Swear words seem to evoke human audience reaction, but would it be appropriate for a robot to repeatedly say the four-letter word? There are jokes involving robots such as a traditional: Question, "How many robots does it take to change a light bulb?" Answer, "Three, one to replace the bulb and two to turn the ladder." Where and when does a robot tell such a joke and to which audience if it is to be funny? What after all is amusing to a robot?

---

[13] Winter Olympics February 2018 demonstrated first robot skiers although they did not do too well.

[14] Carl Benedict Frey and Michael A. Osborne, *The Future of Employment,* Oxford Dept. Engineering, September 17, 2013.

Of course, after humans are replaced, computers would only have to make jokes with each other and so would probably understand them, especially because in their data bank, they would have heard them all before. But would they then laugh? In a similar vein, will there be robotic psychiatrists, where a person enters their symptoms and the machine tells them whether they are bipolar or not? Forget data entry and do patients just tell the robot about problems while sitting on its couch? How many humans will want to spend six years studying medicine and then at least three years more on psychiatry in order to compete with a factory-produced and programmed robot?

Taking the concept of jokes further, obviously a protected job will be for comedians because it is otherwise hard to imagine a robot standing in front of an audience making it laugh by telling robot jokes. The AI could pick from a list of every joke ever told, but it still must make it funny to an audience and a lot of humor is in delivery and playing the audience. But then again, possibly Robin Williams already did that in *Bicentennial Man*, even with a dead-pan robotic face.[15] The point here being whether eventually robots become sentient,[16] will it ever be possible to program in emotion such as if one considers parental love for a child it has created? Without procreation, can a robot even have the same level of feeling?

A further area possibly requiring ongoing human interface would be in regard to carrying out negotiations. If two sides are trying to reach a compromise, many techniques are involved. The ultimate favored solution is technically where both sides have a *win-win*[17] conclusion, each gaining the ultimate satisfaction. Perhaps, this is what computers could deliver having managed to calculate all possibilities and coming up with a compromise. On the other hand, in the real world, one side usually hopes

---

[15] Film in which some android endeavors to become human, gradually acquiring emotions, 1999.

[16] Sentient beings have capacity to feel, perceive, or experience subjectively, said to be composed of the five aggregates: matter, sensation, perception, mental formations, and consciousness.

[17] Roger Fisher and William Ury, *Getting to Yes*, Penguin, 1981. Credited as all-time best seller business book by *Business Week,* but while presenting many good ideas, relies heavily on proceeding until the other side gives in with a "Yes," ignoring cultural variations where a Yes can also mean Perhaps, or even a No.

to get an advantage and earn the best possible percentage on a transaction, rather than just settling for the most equitable outcome for both sides. Apply the principal to stock markets, and theoretically, there would be no gains or losses if a system could already predict price movements in advance. Trading floors have largely seen many humans replaced as computers match trades.

Journalism was suggested as a profession that might be resilient, but it is easy to see that this is fast disappearing with the many blogs published by thousands of individuals with shared agency distribution and where everyone with a mobile phone is now a potential reporter. There will always be the need for actual journalists, only that there will be fewer possibilities and their numbers reduced. On the other hand, people producing comics may have an extended life where original one-off ideas and drawings are required. With the enormous salaries paid to anchor personalities on TV, there must be a robotic replacement already out there on the drawing board waiting to replace them. But, where journalists speculate on outcomes, for the second year in a row, Unanimous AI's artificial *swarm* intelligence has predicted TIME's Person of the Year with 100 percent success rate, proving it can take in human insight in real-time to optimize choice.[18]

In real life, people tend to adapt, capable of shifting toward one idea in favor of another as more information comes in, so in this TIME's case, AI's artificial swarm intelligence, known as UNU, was capable of this kind of adjustment. The process is getting really near human adaptation or group thinking, rather than sticking to a set programmed path. Unanimous' AI founder and CEO, Louis Rosenberg, explained how swarm AI worked by combining real-time human input with algorithms to produce what he called an *emergent hive mind*. This system tends to be smarter than regular AI or an individual human. Overall, it is the way a swarm AI can optimize decision making while relying on human insight that is available in real time, making the technology particularly impressive. Forecasting using swarm AI technology is all about generating optimized outcome probabilities for the various alternatives by weighting competing

---

[18] References: www.unanimous.ai

sets of information and converging on solutions that maximize the populations' collective confidence. This, Rosenberg explained, means that,
as world events changed in real time, the *swarming* algorithms allow
forecasts to adapt, converging on updated probabilities. This is a really
important advancement to be considered in the future where a computer
program can predict voting for Trump as the *Person of the Year*, reflecting
not necessarily reality, but how people might vote, hence emerging a real
human interface.

Take this further and there is the development of quantum computers that take the swarm concept further by being able to come in with
multiple values, make sense of these, and then come up with a single
result from of all of them. This can be likened to having to equate what
Christmas presents to buy for a large family building in preferences, what
each person might like, how favored the individual is by others in the
family, what they own already, and so on, and then work this in within an
allowable budget. Where computers started by handling basically math-
ematical applications, based on 0s and 1s, quantum computers use the
multiple laser technology. Their use now is in its infancy, so consequently,
long-term applications cannot be really comprehended beyond saying
the development is as it was with the leap from punch card sorters to
computers.

So, while complete jobs are being lost to AI, some will, at the same
time, at least in the short run, be enhanced through the IT interface.
The journalists might simply rely on the *swarm* technology for their
predictions. Surgery is being assisted by machines that carry out many
operations more successfully than humans do, and perhaps, the AI can
predict complications that might follow in future from a genetic finger-
print. AI can also reduce time and cost and a robot does not need to go
on annual leave. Partial self-diagnosis can remove some of the inevitable
time needed to wait in a doctor's waiting room for the appointments. At
the most elementary school level, Google allows students to check on data
without going to the library to searching for the text. Lecturers already
use programs to check their students' plagiarism. The problem with all
of this is that a stage seems inevitable where the machine will be able to
do the surgery, but the surgeon will never have to train to be able to do
the job in the first place. The surgeon will be replaced by the computer

programmer designing the task. Either way, the jobs are inevitably on the way out, and this will be likely within a short timeframe. A catch-up here is that where machines conduct things such as surgery, there will need to be a 100 percent reliable backup power system to drive the AI. If power fails during an operation or a machine fails, in future, there will not be a trained human surgeon sitting around waiting to take over.

The danger in all of this is that people become statistics. Just as with the argument for automatic cars, that overall they save more lives, if they get a few wrong that is better than the alternative. If a robotic operation goes wrong, is this just written off as an aberration? This becomes personal if the individual becomes one of those statistics.

For those who remain employed, one can only guess at percentages with only a small number becoming entrepreneurs, some as artists and performers, others simply as intellectuals, social volunteers, and religious preachers telling us what to expect after death. Those left will need to still have some form of income to survive: what do they live on?

Having talked about the jobs that will disappear, this also needs to be taken in the context of the ever-increasing population expansion. When the current literature suggests 30 percent or even 60 percent of jobs being lost in a short timeframe, they are talking of the unemployment figures at a particular date so that in fact the absolute numbers of jobs that disappear will be even greater. Whether loss of jobs would encourage individuals to have fewer children or not is a debatable point, given they will have so much more free time, and the Malthus[19] postulates that population would decrease as food sources became scarcer, with an increased population did not come to fruition. The Swiss UBI referendum, which was defeated, suggested one rate of payment for adults and another for children, so this concept could drive higher procreation so as to provide an income stream as some existing welfare systems already do.

On the other hand, with the current world population of 7.6 billion expected to reach 8.6 billion in 2030 (30 percent job loss at that level would be 2.58 billion estimated on total not working population), 9.8 billion in 2050 (or 30 percent job loss 2.94 billion), and 11.2 billion

---

[19] Thomas Robert Malthus, *An Essay on the Principle of Population*, 1798.

in 2100[20] (30 percent job loss 3.36 billion), it could be that something might have to give way, where, for example, even if people did not run out of food, they could run out of water.[21] In other words, by 2100, at say only 30 percent unemployed, this is bad enough, but what if this unemployment has hit 60 percent by that time representing 6.72 billion unemployed,[22] a number compared to almost the overall population of the earth today? Will there be food and water sufficient to keep everyone alive, let alone with an income? Yet, with every negative, there is always at least a little positive hope because fresh water could come from desalination plants, and in 2017, China-engineered rice, which will grow in salt water. Should man in future decide that there was not enough room for raising or passion for eating animals, human ingenuity has already come up with meat substitutes that even taste like meat and where no animal is killed. Looking at a glass half full, rather than half empty, there could perhaps still be hope.

---

[20] UN Department of Economic and Social Affairs, *World Population Prospects: The 2017 Revision,* June 2017.

[21] Cape Town, South Africa, in January 2018 is predicted to run out of water.

[22] Unemployed includes all people needing sustenance to survive.

CHAPTER 4

Prospects for New Jobs

The bad news is that humans can see how most of their current jobs are on the way out. On the other hand, there may be some good news where AI itself lends to the creation of new jobs. Unfortunately, as with all technology, it is hard to define all the new job possibilities that might not have even been thought of. Either way, following recent trends, there will likely be a heavier focus on short-term jobs, rather than for past long-term employment.

On the global market, new jobs need to be considered on a global scale, where, for example, jobs might be lost in Australia or the United States, but as happens now, created by outsourcing in India or the Philippines.[1] In the longer term, this labor market will equalize as the cost of services balances out with the market finding costs the same in all countries. Some countries will see winners, and other countries will be losers.

Eventually, most commerce will be mixed. With the ease of transmitting data, there is the situation where one major Australian newspaper is completely set up daily in Bangladesh to then be returned electronically for local printing in Australia. With the different size of populations by country, it will be some time before labor equalizes. In the meantime, jobs are created in some countries to the detriment of others. King Canute realized that some things are impossible to change,[2] while others might still believe that they can retreat behind national borders.[3]

The new application for jobs will obviously be in the AI area including robotics, with the need for programmers and coders. Robots require three things: mobility, dexterity, and autonomous perception.[4] Unfortunately,

---

[1] Large.

[2] An apocryphal anecdote illustrating the piety or humility.

[3] Trump dismantling Free Trade Agreements.

[4] Dom Galeon, CNBC Boston Dynamics, November 15, 2017.

ultimately, the machines will be able to program themselves, but this is still some way off for all applications. What is available, however, are systems that allow us to reach all the information of the world, and AI will let us interface with that information. Now what is needed is people who know how to access that data and what to do with it. They will also need to be able to ensure that all the options are programmed into an equation and no gaps remain, so we need to be able to understand logic and relevance. This will require a massive amount of input initially, but eventually will possibly come up with a universal accessible data body, such as an AI Wikipedia, which could be accessed and built into any system program without having to be built separately for each application. This is similar to *time share* on existing computers but could be simultaneous. The rest of the problem then becomes in determining the right questions to ask.

Policing will likely create more jobs because an increased physical presence will be needed to control the rising masses of unemployed who have time on their hands to revolt. Evidence of this is already obvious. Police presence would be heavily supplemented by AI or robotics with surveillance applications among these. Increasingly, areas are monitored by CCTV (and drones), and while this will continue for now, it still requires a human to interpret what is seen. As soon as that is said, new systems monitor and respond to CCTV, notifying police when, for example, an intruder is lurking before a crime is committed. That and when systems suggest the possibility of an attack before it happens. The emphasis is on crime prevention by pointing out to the public that anyone committing a crime is sure to be caught. Demonstrating an advance in this technology, China, in October 2017, opened the first fully automated police station.

The introduction of drones and their use is still an infant industry, with many more applications not yet conceived. On the one hand, their introduction will reduce some jobs, but they will require many operators on applications, ranging from real estate photography, entertainment, and rescue services,[5] as well as in underwater surveillance, on goods or for mail delivery. Drones are also used to spray crops, survey pipelines and power cables, and in firefighting. However, once again, programs already

---

[5] First-ever rescue by a drone conducted in NSW Australia, January 18, 2018.

set drones on pre-planned routes not requiring operators, and while some systems require handlers, Amazon has been granted a patent for drone delivery technology that allows the craft to strategically self-destruct in the event of an emergency. The system uses the drone's onboard computer to determine the safest course of action.

The technology that allows people sitting in the United States to fly an aircraft in a far-away country to target designated terrorists could also be used for pilotless passenger aircraft. The main reason this is not currently used is for the comfort of passengers who like to know there is a human up front flying the plane, when in reality, commercial pilots in the main are only involved in flying during take-off and landing, an estimated time of around seven minutes. Even then with automated take-off and landing systems, they often just have to look on. Again, jobs to be lost on planes. Pilots on the ground do not have to worry about jet lag, but who wants to be on a plane a pilot could crash without risk to themselves after a domestic or a religious epiphany? The time will, however, come when passengers will not be told if there is anyone up front, just as they are currently lied to when told to switch off mobile phones for *security reasons*, when this is simply to prevent problems for mobile companies with high-speed switching between mobile towers.[6]

With all the free time people will have without jobs, there is a vast opportunity for providing an AI interface to fill this void. The gaming industry and virtual reality is one such area, as will be the need for fitness trainers to get people out of the home, or in teaching AI itself and how to develop hobbies for the ample new spare time.

While jobs in department stores will disappear, online marketing and delivery systems will increase where one is able to buy a product from the other side of the world and have it delivered within two days while able to track its movement on your phone. The phone itself is already a halfway house to the next development where already it is possible to talk to a watch.

There are reports that robots are now able to *cook* and are certainly able to prepare food, clear tables, and it is said, serve as well as any

---

[6] Low-flying aircraft at speed requires mobile signals to jump from one tower to next, and this can scramble signals.

waitress. Presumably, robots will be able to imitate the taste. It is difficult to see how one would program the required *heat* of a curry or what something smells like, but it is likely someone will manage this. While people can still afford to eat out, this is likely to continue, and outside catering should increase if people are moved to smaller housing in urban centers.

As people live longer, provided they are permitted to, or want to, the increase in age-care jobs will spiral. Certainly, robots can help and even become *friends* with humans, but do robots come around for a cup of tea and a chat? It also becomes questionable whether anyone would want even a remedial massage from a robot. It remains likely that, before some person dies, at death bed, a human touch would be appreciated.[7] Who knows, however, if burial or *body disposal* will also not become automated?

There will also be jobs in *virtual zoos*, given that more animals become extinct, remembering the song predicting, *Tree museum*.[8] The idea leads to other forms of historic interaction concepts that will be required to fill people's extra free time.

While the movie *Water World* with Kevin Costner was noted as a box office flop, humanity has only started to explore the possibilities of floating cities and utilization of the world's oceans. These floating concepts will need to be staffed, and a whole new industry is waiting.

There is likely to be further development around new forms of energy storage. Some of this will be around existing technology, such as solar panels and wind farms, but it is likely new methods will also emerge as storage batteries improve or a better form of delivery is invented.

Space travel will open possibilities not yet even dreamed of. Answering the question of why go off planet, the answer is possibly "because it is there, we can, or eventually because humanity must do so."[9] What this will open up is, so far beyond the current comprehension, any speculation is only that. However, it could lead to overall implications for the global economy where say gold or some other valuable or unknown mineral is

---

[7] A Japanese man has officially married a robot.

[8] Mentioned in the *Big Yellow Taxi* song by *Counting Crows* for time when nature has disappeared.

[9] The author was sent to bed without supper by his father in the 1960s after making an *outrageous* statement that men would soon visit the moon.

found in large quantities on some other planet, let alone the discovery of *intelligent life*. There may be a need to establish off-planet colonies in case some virus[10] overtakes planet earth, or some asteroid wants to collide. Follow science fiction and reality is often not far behind. In the overall scheme of space, travel possibilities open for new jobs. Unfortunately, these would be for highly trained individuals coming from a small portion of the population. The real problem will be for the lesser *skilled* and what training and ability they need to hold a job.

With all the complicated new technology introduced by AI, there will be a need for people to have jobs trying to teach others how all this works. This is coaching outside what is generally now taught at schools where curricula have difficulty keeping up. There needs to be some reskilling into programming and something like *a Nano* designer focus. There will always be the need for people who can think *creatively*, and this is a definable skill set in itself. To encourage this, it can be seen how advanced tech companies, such as those based in Silicon Valley, have *Open offices* and free workspaces, not your conventional layouts, their spaces designed to allow free flow of thought. Google executives are ferried to and from work in driverless cars,[11] all part of trying to create forward thinking.

With pressure on living space as the planet reaches its nine billion projected inhabitants, it is likely that accommodation will change. As can be seen, for example, in Japan, some people are already staying in small *cubicles* fitted out with all comforts of home. This small space has most of the possible conveniences of a full-fledged apartment for people in which to sleep, watch TV, read, or have their Wi-Fi while the rest of their life is conducted in public space or at work. In the United States, a scheme was recently proposed for designed *Hexagonal pods* to be provided as an accommodation for the homeless in an overcrowded New York, with no more available land. These pods would be raised up on scaffolds and attached to the outside of existing buildings.[12]

---

[10] Medical experts think the world is due for another global pandemic within 50 years. Professor of Medicine at Queen's University, Dr. Gerald A. Evans, November 20, 2017.

[11] As of November 2017, the cars are on auto, but still require a human behind the wheel.

[12] Kyree Leary, Framlab, @ KyreeLeary.

As part of intensified proximity living, laundry goes to a laundromat and food and drink is purchased hot or cold from machines. People just crawl into their little cubicles to sleep where they store basic possessions and otherwise just use common space. Even cubical ownership might change and instead be rented out on an Airbnb basis to generate income. Also, if the long-term trend is toward ride share, rather than car ownership, the concept of parking spaces will need to change and fewer if any people will need driving licenses. Again, licensing inspectors will disappear. In car parks now, there is no longer a need for parking tickets and instead number plate photo recognition calculates how long you stay and charges accordingly. The police also do away with registration stickers and rely on similar technology.

Fighting the backlash over new jobs not replacing the old, one of the first things employers should look at is making the existing workplaces more productive. The labor regulations that have developed over the years have driven the speed to automation. After the expense of buying and installing a machine, beyond routine maintenance, it does not have four weeks annual paid leave, sick leave, emergency leave, maternity leave, days off for public holidays, does not waste time looking on Facebook, and while eventually, a robot may require upgrading, does not qualify for paid long service leave nor strike. Neither are there the administrative costs of payroll management and payroll tax. Consequently, employers take the opportunity to automate wherever possible. The positive aspect in this is that it creates a scope for a rise in consultancy jobs showing businesses how technology can replace jobs.

Ray Kurzweil, Google's Chief Engineer and one of the current most notable futurists, stated that there is no worry about job losses in the future and has continued by stating that almost all his predictions have been within a small margin of error.[13] Except he then admits, in relation to the Uber phenomenon, this caught him by surprise. That of course is one of the major issues with projections, where even the experts get it wrong. If someone gets one thing wrong, how reliable are their other predictions? If someone makes many predictions, it is then possible to just

---

[13] Speaking to *Fortune*, Ray Kurzweil dismissed most people's worries about automation, 2017.

focus on the few out of many which came to fruition. Even Nostradamus has been shown to be wrong with events seen to be selected to fit his predictions.[14] If someone is famous because they became a film star or TV personality acting out someone else's words, does that make their economic predictions or presidential aspirations relevant? The point is that, in the future, at the speed that AI is developing, it is almost impossible to predict what might be possible and so-called experts also get it wrong. Add to that where inventions themselves might be hypothetical for events not yet envisaged, as revealed at the recent January 2018 Las Vegas CES Technology show, where the Spartan company have brought out men's silver thread-lined cotton underwear to protect testicles against Wi-Fi and similar electronic signals from radiation. Men using their laptops on their laps might not have been aware this threat even exists.

Against the increased likelihood of job losses is the rear-guard action being fought against progress, but that assists job retention. One example here is the pursuit against Uber mainly in developed countries where established taxi cartels have curtailed the ride share services. On the other hand, in less developed countries, the Uber concept has advanced exponentially for cars with the concept extended to motor bikes in some countries. A person can have an Uber account set up in one country and still use the app to book a driver in America, Hong Kong, or even Vietnam, while at the same time, not even knowing an address for the pickup point, which appears on the driver's screen. In poor countries, anyone with a motor bike and a mobile phone can be in work, and no one seems to mind wearing a passenger helmet after hundreds have worn it previously.

The attack on Uber, because it is cheaper to operate than having to buy a taxi plate license, is justified on that basis, if not on almost all other accounts. Uber vehicles are inspected, insurance needs to be obtained, drivers' details are up there for passengers to see, and there is the option where they can rate a driver after each trip. Passengers can see what star rating a driver has and how many trips have previously been made. Drivers dropping below a set rating are computer-banned from further app access. None of this can be obtained for your normal taxi. There have

---

[14] Michel de Nostradame, 16th century French apothecary and reputed seer.

been many cases of bad behavior from taxi drivers, which hardly hit the news, yet Uber drivers appear targeted by the media.

Airbnb, as in accommodation type sharing, will also increase as people find it more convenient to share than to own, opening other job opportunities. Once again, the regulators are hard on the track of taxing and curtailing this development.

Governments also try and featherbed their own employees to try and keep unemployment figures down. This also provides a source of jobs for the lesser-trained individuals who would otherwise clog up the welfare system. With these jobs, you have people sweeping streets, writing parking tickets, and mounting toll booths when these jobs could easily be automated.

Yet, when looking for a job, how does one overcome the computer systems that are increasingly involved in job selection? Most professional recruiters currently feed CVs into programs and have them identify those CVs that tick all the pre-programmed boxes. The remainder go into the trash. So, someone who knows how that programming works might remain employed where the lesser skilled stay unemployed. Perhaps, geniuses, like Einstein, might not like ticking boxes and their skills are missed. Otherwise, people will need to learn how the computer makes the job selection and feed into that.

While new jobs are likely to be created even in areas not yet thought of, the difficult part is that these are again unlikely to be among the uneducated and structural poor who somehow will still need to be looked after if they are allowed to survive. That is, if the planet itself allows it and global warming does not end life itself.

CHAPTER 5

Climate Change

In predicting an unknown future, *climate change* plays a large part in the guess work. Here, it is necessary to separate the difference between climate change absolute, as climate has been changing since the earth began, from man-made contribution to changing climate.[1] Having made the distinction, the fact that climate change appears to influence living conditions, this will influence job losses while perhaps providing some opportunities.

To put this in perspective in regard to its effect on employment, NASA's Goddard Space Flight Center satellite data reports an 80mm rise in sea levels between 1993 and 2017, or 3.2mm a year (±0.4), with the last two years falling off.

What this means in relation to job losses is difficult to determine, but starting with the lands that are only slightly above the sea level, there are many islands in the Pacific that are likely to be eventually covered with rising water levels, although at present, the danger is more about increasing weather changes. This is exacerbated by ever-increasing populations, which reduce the living areas and make it difficult to dispose of rubbish.[2] In addition, during storms, some islands are washed over by heavy seas and conditions might ultimately necessitate the population moving elsewhere.[3]

---

[1] As early as 1896, scientist Svante Arrhenius calculated that doubling the concentration of carbon dioxide in the atmosphere would raise earth's temperature between 8 and 9 degrees Celsius.

[2] Some of the small island systems, such as on tiny Tuvalu, have massive rubbish dumps that cannot be disposed of or dumped in the sea.

[3] Also, difficulty of U.S. deposited plutonium in *Runit Dome* of Marshall Islands capable of seepage into ocean.

Other countries such as Vietnam, Indonesia, Bangladesh, and China with large populations in river delta areas are particularly vulnerable. Unfortunately, in many cases, the living conditions in these areas have worsened with people upstream cutting down trees and natural vegetation to make room for housing, which, in turn, has then been constructed in flood and risk-prone areas.

The discussion here always gets back to timeframes on AI introduction and the eventual need for UBI initiation. If for now considering an endpoint 100-year projection, accepting hypothetical available job losses on a 30-, 60-, 80-, or 100-year timeframes, even a 3.2mm a year water level rise could have a corresponding survival crisis, let alone job loss effect. In that, climate change job losses will correspond to denser living in urban centers with shared facilities. This population concentration will bring with it technology to suit. An example is where digital printers are reducing in price and are predicted to be able to create any inanimate object, with the result that it will soon be possible to print off a *Big Mac and Fries* at home quicker than an *Uber Eats* drone could deliver. The rise in prefabricated structures will proliferate, and even *laser-printed* buildings are replacing traditional concepts.

On the down side will be the loss of jobs if water levels sweep away areas used for agriculture, while, on the plus side, a whole new generation of climate scientists will be required to design structurally resilient accommodation and work out how the urban masses will survive.

Out of the change, it is likely to see a global move instigated by governments, as in China where people living in the *hutongs* were moved to high-rise apartments. The design of these new structures as housing of the future are likely to require major redesign. The peasant farmer with no rice land left needs to be provided for by government. Looking at the thousands of new small apartments in high-rise buildings all over Hong Kong and the neighboring islands, the demand for infrastructure such as for waste water treatment presents requirement for massive processing works, but requires few laborers. This future concept is demonstrated with the Green High Technology concept city of Songdo, an hour's travel from Seoul, the capital of Korea. The city is based on buildings around a central communal park so that no one needs to walk more than 30 minutes from their residence to shopping or their place of work. Consequently, there is no need for cars. Rubbish is no longer collected, but goes through tubes to a central recycling and disposal unit. Jobs are centralized and reduced wherever possible.

Looking in rice paddies, tractors are handling planting in a day, which would have previously taken 100 people to do. The majority of peasants replaced need to head for the cities, and even if water levels rise, it is easier to protect the one tractor driver and his family than the former 100 rice growers. Eventually, the machine will not even require its driver to plan or harvest rice.

On top of any actual rises in water levels, indications are that the planet is warming up on the surface. This will also have an impact as people attempt to stay cooler, and older people might not respond well to higher temperatures.

The essential point overall will be that climate changing elements, which themselves are unpredictable, will add another dimension to already increasing job losses. Whichever way the problem is addressed, it appears inevitable that unemployment will continue to rise. Overall, however, the people without jobs will still need some means of survival. The big question remains, how this can be achieved.

CHAPTER 6

Universal or Unconditional Basic Income

To address the seemingly inevitable loss of jobs on a global scale, the concept of a universal basic income (UBI) (sometimes called *unconditional income, guaranteed income*, or *social credit*) has been suggested.[1] The idea is that every citizen must have sufficient money on which to survive, so whether having paid employment or not, they would be given a set annual amount irrespective of means test, and this would be funded by the government through taxes and earnings from publicly owned enterprises. The concept is that it is necessary to keep people at least alive. Initially, UBI was perceived as a stabilization mechanism, but later, it has come to be recognized that increased job losses will be inevitable, and so a payment needed to cater for this. One payment, it was considered would be easier to administer than the current social welfare systems that exist adjusted for income, unemployment, disability, child endowment, regional location, and so on. So far, various countries have experimented with the UBI concept.

In recent developments, the Swiss under their legal system put a countrywide UBI idea to a referendum in 2016 and it was defeated on a 76 percent *no* vote.

The Finnish government is now running a two-year trial from 2017, as is Ontario in Canada.

The Dutch City of Utrecht from 2017 also launched testing, experimenting with different levels of aid, as has Barcelona in Spain. In Alaska, they have found it possible to launch the Permanent Fund from their oil revenues. Otherwise, there have been experiments on restricted fronts

---

[1] In 1963, Robert Theobald published the book *Free Men and Free Markets*, advocating a guaranteed minimum income.

such as within a system covering several villages in India, Uganda, with eight NGOs launching a fund providing income to 56 adults in Fort Portal, and Brazil with the *Bolsa Familia program*, a means-tested assistance for the poor. Namibia uses a *Basic Income Grant (BIG),* while Kenya with the *Give Direct* program has the longest modern Western scheme of its type. The base idea in most experiments is that the UBI replaces all other welfare payments, and hence makes it simpler to operate welfare payments at a lesser cost.

These initiatives have value as experiments, but when taken in isolation for small pockets of people, they do not help address the question of *universal* where they only become extensions of a welfare system funded by a specific entity. These are piecemeal solutions that do not really connect with the main stream of a country's economic structure because the benefits are simply paid out of normal revenue, rather than through an overall country economic model.

Google's former China President, Kai-Fu Lee, has agreed on job losses to the extent that he believed that half human jobs will be lost in the next decade and he also expressed the importance of retraining to help the displaced human worker adapt to relevant professions. He is not so keen on UBI,[2] thinking that it will not work if people do not have an incentive.

On the other hand, many well-respected individuals, including economics, Nobel laureates, and tech billionaires like Virgin Group CEO Richard Branson and Tesla CEO and founder Elon Musk, have considered UBI to be a potentially viable economic solution that could cushion the effects of inevitable unemployment due to automation. The missing link remains, however, how to pay for it. Equally important is something no government appears willing to address, in how this will by default, reconstruct the political landscape.

UBI trials currently ongoing might be recent experiments, but China from the Mao revolution adopted the Iron Rice Bowl principle.[3] This

---

[2] *CNBC's Squawk Box*, November 13, 2017.

[3] Iron rice bowl (simplified Chinese: 铁饭碗; traditional Chinese: 鐵飯碗; pinyin: tiě fàn wǎn) is a term used to refer to an occupation with guaranteed job security for life, including income and benefits. https://en.wikipedia.org/wiki/Iron_rice_bowl

followed the nationalization of all factories into state-owned enterprises (SOEs), after which their staff in effect all became government employees, and hence were guaranteed employment for life. Not only that, but if a worker died, a relative could move into the deceased's job. The system of support from cradle to grave saw the SOEs providing medical support from pregnancy through childbirth and into old age. Unfortunately, as there was no individual incentive for workers to perform, as was found with farm laborers under pure *commune-ism*, it did not take long for factory workers to realize that, if you received the same reward as the next person who was lazy and did no work, it was pointless to work harder. Within the political machinery, when setting output for state corporation targets, it became customary to report successful outcomes, rather than achieving them.

To address the burdens these policies were placing on the country and its ability to pay, under Deng Xiaoping in China, it was finally decided that something needed to be done to increase productivity. The government from 1980 decided that iron rice bowls should be dismantled and divorced from SOEs. However, the policy was not applied to government employees outside the SOEs. In then attempting to *commercialize* these factories under a revised constitution scrapping the planned economy in favor of a *socialist market economy* with *Chinese characteristics*, this proved extremely difficult. Some of these government corporations still had up to 60 percent of retired employees on the payroll. If an SOE wanted to be equitized or privatized, few buyers wanted to accept that burden, and so the government had to take over the retirees. The SOE debt had to be written off, and with no other pension schemes, someone had to keep paying the retired workers.[4]

In the necessary restructuring and reduction of padded employee numbers within the SOEs, as increasingly workers became unemployed unsettling the population, it was difficult for the government to address the sheer size of the transition, and new welfare measures adopted tended to be stop-gap solutions leading to the present disorganized policies. In the population, there are estimated 40 million more men than women,

---

[4] Author involvement as consultant in process across China on EU funded project, 1998–2000.

and the strict one-child policy has had to be reversed[5] because of the strain on one couple (or none) having to support (and fund) two sets of non-superannuated grandparents. These situations may be currently peculiar to China, but offer lessons for the future when considering a UBI needing to fund retirees in an aging population that at the same time lives longer.

For now, China has its own form of social insurance scheme, which it built in little more than 10 years, but coverage while expanding rapidly remains inconsistent, inadequate, inefficient, and often riddled with corruption.[6] The problem is exacerbated due to China's aforementioned aging population with its working-age population continuing to shrink. Minimum income guarantees have been rolled out to the countryside, benefiting more than 50 million residents in impoverished areas. Since dismantling the overall rice bowl concept, from 10 years ago where just over 200 million people had pensions, mostly in the cities, now almost 700 million are covered in one way or another. Again, the payments are linked to geographic residency and can vary considerably on both income and medical coverage having flat-lined in recent years as the country attempts to balance the financial model. The outcome has been that there is not just one social welfare program but many, all of which are different. The complication here is that, with a move of the rural population to urban areas, while there might be meager coverage for an individual in the country, this does not apply if they move to the city where costs are higher. Overall, the system is one that is difficult to understand, inflexible, and lacks equality, suggesting that, over time, welfare will need to standardize and here a UBI might be the answer.

Historically, there is a pattern of progression from Chinese experience, which can be studied if there is eventually to be the need for a UBI, whether in China or elsewhere. The freeing of state enterprises from unrestrained financial support leads to disproportionate unemployment and political discontent that the government could not allow. Consequently, they had to adopt *Band-Aid* solutions because it was not possible to afford to do everything at once with a resulting piecemeal solution aimed at specific gaps. Government officials had to be covered first and

---

[5] Canceled in October 2015 after 37 years of restriction.
[6] Tania Branigan, *The Guardian*, April 23, 2017.

then benefits for regional necessity, all of which have resulted in the complicated situation as exists today. The Chinese government continues to fill the identified gap, but there remains danger that the system that still covers the government officials for life, but not the remainder, eventually finishes with a two-tiered society. In this, while the government appears to mostly have its population under control by quashing all dissent, and what opposition there is rarely reaches outside the press,[7] there remains the danger of social instability laying the groundwork for possible grass-roots uprisings.[8] So far, the central authorities have managed to stem any open discontent, but the split-level social welfare system has long been a dilemma for government.

It needs to be remembered also that, because there is already a global economy, what happens when one country has fully adopted a UBI will affect other countries not yet at the point of needing one to be introduced.

Overall, however, the principle of having to introduce some payment to all unemployed appears inevitable, and it is unlikely that, once implemented, it would ever be reversed. Once people have a taste of never having to work (at jobs they do not like), they are unlikely to want to be put back on the grind mill. At the same time, they might not respond well to being on the bottom of the income stream. As one of the wealthiest men in Indonesia once said, "I have been lucky and have much wealth but if I do not appear to be helping the poor, one day they might just come and take it all away from me."[9]

---

[7] Bureaus such as CNN have to clear stories with the Chinese government to maintain their country accreditation.

[8] Hughes, Neil C. *Smashing the Iron Rice Bowl.* Foreign Affairs. January 28, 2009. Accessed April 09, 2017. https://foreignaffairs.com/articles/asia/1998-07-01/smashing-iron-rice-bowl

[9] Interview by author with "Mr. William," owner Astra Corporation, 1985.

CHAPTER 7

Benefits of a UBI

It is easy to paint a picture of the Garden of Eden where no one must work or exert themselves, where there is sufficient disposable income to live comfortably while *government* provides everything else. A great dream, but whether this holds up in reality?

Some people just like to write books, and as most of them will admit, they are not doing this for the huge income it grants them. These people would be content on UBI. The musician doing it for the love of music would be in the same boat. People who get joy from helping others for very little reward could keep on doing this. Heads of some religions would accept this easily. There would be more time to pursue hobbies. In the first two categories, the problem is that artificial intelligence will soon be writing those books, creating the music, and playing it. Helping people emotionally might make such jobs last a little longer even if the handicapped now can receive more assistance from mechanical intervention, but even that could disappear. Would anyone countenance robot psychiatrists?

There will always be some people with an inquisitive mind looking at the impossible or improbable, so presumably life goes on. The main problem is when there are massive numbers of undereducated and unskilled humans who will still need money to live on, but might otherwise have nothing to do.

Under benefits of being in work, many advertisements tell that work is good for health and well-being and contributes to happiness, building confidence, and self-esteem while rewarding financially. The opposite must imply that it is bad for health and well-being and makes people unhappy. Obviously, these concepts are fine, but there is also the financial reward from work, which does not need to be overlooked. Do people need work for health? What if a universal basic income (UBI) could be financed and equitably delivered, allowing everyone to keep on living without needing to have a job. How does this effect health?

Under the concept of humanity, governments of earth could not allow masses of people to starve and one only needs to revert to the photos of the last Great Depression to see how desperate people's lives became when they did not have enough money on which to live. Remember also that living in a developed world requires a base level of expenditure for services, as well as food for a base level of contentment. UBI, even if it does not meet all expectations, at least allows people to survive. It also has a communal benefit because the alternative of large numbers of unemployed, not just the 25 percent as per the depression era, but around say 80 percent where without a basic sum of money to live on, this would lead to anarchy. Would a UBI prevent potential chaos?

Provided a UBI could be practical, and the majority of people do not have to work for pay, there is the possibility that people might still like to work in their now un-job-related daily routine and contribute to society in other ways. Many people have hobbies they might be happy to follow full time and be content with this.

The stark reality in the benefit of a UBI introduction falls on the need to keep unemployed individuals sufficiently content with enough money so that they will not revolt against authority and challenge their governments.

CHAPTER 8

Shortcomings of a UBI

What does not seem to be recognized by UBI proponents is in what Keynes recognized many years ago in *paying people to dig ditches and then filling them up again*, that in the digging, these people had a job and were doing something whether useful or not. It occupied their time. Under a UBI, people are not expected to perform any work. There is a subtle difference in doing something, even if it is useless, as against doing nothing at all.

The issue was eloquently addressed by the Moynihan Report where noted economist Daniel Moynihan under the Lyndon Johnson administration aiming at the plight of what was still permitted to be called *black people*. He argued that, without access to jobs and the means to contribute meaningful support to a family, black men would become systematically alienated from their roles as husbands and fathers. This, he postulated, would cause increasing rates of divorce, child abandonment, and out-of-wedlock births, as well as other associated antisocial behaviors.

While his attention was on the then black community, the *access to jobs* reference can be applied to the population as a whole, at the same time highlighting how segments within the community can be affected differently. What, for example, will be the job loss rate among genders, will women be better at the sort of jobs that disappear last, requiring interpersonal contact, rather than men, and what then is the outcome of a heavy bias in gender unemployment? How about societies where women are already kept in the home for child rearing and women's jobs go? How does this affect expansion of and integration of a multi-cultural society, or does it lead to a Tower of Babel?[1]

---

[1] In Genesis following Great Flood designed to unite humanity, but eventually fell apart.

If it is agreed that jobs will go, with each new advancement replacing jobs, there will need to be adjustments. Some of these adjustments will be beneficial. Others will try and curtail progress, such as from those who believed that the earth was flat and were prepared to execute anyone who tried to suggest the contrary. Religion, which was invented by primitives to try and make sense of the age-old question of, "What are we doing here?" or "What is the purpose of life" and to give comfort to the dying, has led to countless arguments over "Which God?" This has led to wars, even when it was the same God on both sides. Religion still acts as a brake on progress where people do not understand that, for example, how the Bible is an allegorical guide to behavior and not an accurate description of what Adam and Eve did in the Garden of Eden. People who established laws supposedly based on instructions from God about what one should eat because food goes bad had at the time no contemplation of refrigeration.

While slowing advancement, religious indoctrination can, at the same time, have beneficial effects to maintain checks and balances. In the religious case, it is establishing a code of behavior, it introduces a heaven and the reward for good (or acceptable) behavior, as against hell to be avoided at all costs. Remove all reward and punishment, and the purpose is eliminated. All that remains is looking after the self. Moving into an IT context, computers have a long way to go before they become emotional. Asimov[2] may have defined the *first law of robotics,* but should a robot kill a person, at the present, they would feel no emotion in doing so. Is it necessary to build a *good* and a *bad* into a robot's program? If so, then who defines the terms?

The simplicity of the robotics law is tested now on many fronts, as demonstrated with experiments in automatic car configuration where a vehicle in case of a pending accident would have to decide between which person is to die. Humans make rational choices, but in an imminent accident, does the automatic car decide to save the baby with a whole life before it or the old man if the car must choose about hitting only one of them? How does a programmer build that in?

---

[2] Isaac Asimov, *Roundabout, Short stories* introducing his "Three Laws of Robotics," *1942.*

While it is known that drones have been used to kill people, there is now controversy regarding drones programmed for killing terrorist targets without human orders. The proposed drones would operate on their own selecting targets and act as pre-programmed independent units. Perhaps, it would be possible to program for them to hold off if there might be a collateral damage, but what defines just what that is and on what variables? Is one accidental death okay, is the limit five kills and how about when humans are used as shields? If it is not acceptable to kill children, at what age is it a child and how is a drone program to know? And then, of course, what about glitches?

All of this relates to what happens when people are on a UBI and how they then choose between what their immediate society considers right and wrong. While working for a paid job, the individuals have to conform to society norms or lose their jobs. Give them a UBI without condition, and they can decide for themselves.

The discussion on all of this interface with computers in regard to right and wrong is as with self-driving cars. Overall, it is argued that if self-drive cars are introduced, even if some mistakes are made, there will be fewer deaths on the road. That postulate might be accurate unless as an individual someone personally becomes one of the statistics that missed out, even if individually they had a perfect driving record.

Attempts have been made to start bringing in a legal framework controlling what robotics can do in future. Organizations have been established to look at the question, such as the Partnership on AI and the Ethics and Governance of AI Fund (IEEE). The problem, of course, is that it is all very well to legislate through some global body (such as the UN) that North Korea disarm its nuclear program, but another to make them do it.[3]

One major issue with a potential UBI, as has been found with other social welfare benefits, is if the purpose is to provide income for all people in a society so they can at least survive in buying food and clothing; how do you stop individuals from wasting this benefit on alcohol, cigarettes, or drugs, leaving no money over for the intended food and having the

---

[3] World leaders met on November 15, 2017, in Manila to discuss this issue.

same problem all over again? The solution tested now in some communities has been to issue the welfare benefit via a credit card that limits what can be purchased similar to use of food stamps. As with any system, some individuals will always try to circumvent the process where some people can stand at supermarkets asking people to buy food with their cards against receiving cash. Arguments posed against the system of cards is that it demonizes a section of the community, and in some cases, has a racist connotation,[4] although overall, the intention is to keep people alive.

These are political as well as computing problems, but at the same time, they interact with a population that might be out of work with nothing to do. Who can know what changes progress will bring? What if smoking *weed* becomes the fashion now legalized in California at end of 2017 and countless people spend their days high on drugs waiting for their next delivery of marijuana by drone? Payment for nothing defies all the laws of contract, but then, perhaps the consideration in the case of a UBI is that the individual's part of the contract is that they sign off not to try and overthrow the government. On the other hand, were a UBI insufficient for all those people out of work, could it simply polarize a two-tier society encouraging a rise against the establishment?

---

[4] Trials made in Australian Aboriginal communities.

CHAPTER 9

Gender Divide

Following the end of the Chinese Communist Party's 19th Congress, the new Politburo Standing Committee was revealed with seven men and as always, no women.[1] Of the 2,280 delegates to Congress, fewer than a quarter were women, prompting the *New York Times* to comment whether China had a women problem? That 25 percent corresponds to numbers of female members and also to numbers of women in China's National Congress.

Further, Times' comment was also that women were less represented the higher up the system went, and at the previous 2012 Congress, only 33 women were appointed on the Central Committee, which elects the Politburo. Only two of the 25 members of the Politburo were women.

Despite Mao's support of women with his *Women hold up half the sky* quotation and acknowledging their importance in the cultural revolution where they were for the first time granted equal status, in reality, women in China still have a long way to go in their fight for equal representation due to institutional factors. One is that, under the Chinese system, one needs to hold local office first before moving up which is difficult from the provincial level where one also needs to build good *guanxi* (connection) to advance. Then, women civil servants retire at 55, while men do at 60.

While the media attack had been on China's recognition of women following the release of the Congress figures, by comparison, there are only 32 percent of MPs in the United Kingdom's House of Commons; they account for only 11 percent of members in India's Lok Sabha and nine percent of Japan's House of Representatives. If worried about low levels of representation in communist countries, in Cuba, women make

---

[1] *Reality check: Does China's Communist Party have a woman problem?* BBC Section Asia, October 25, 2017.

up 49 percent of the *Asamblea Nacional*. For democracies, women make up 26 percent of Angela Merkel's CDU party in Germany and around 30 percent of Theresa May's Conservatives in the United Kingdom.

While from the foregoing it can be seen how politically women in the main are unrepresented, in relation to continuing job losses and an eventual society that might evolve, there does not appear to be a specific focus for or against women under different types of political systems. That is, democracy might have a showing of 33 percent of women, but some communist societies display more. There remains, however, this slant against women's representation in China, which might cause later concern.

As with all futuristic planning, nothing can be certain, and with the rise of AI, it might be that women are more suited for the jobs of the future and better able to adjust their temperament to working with robots, being less aggressive and not testosterone-fueled. The main consideration regarding women's role would still be the rate of child births, and whether this will be permitted to continue as naturally as possible, permitting in-vitro fertilization on demand, or whether governments will curtail child birth if in their power. Alternatively, will there be, as in Singapore, special incentives for people to have children with higher achievement profiles or implementation of some human engineering to meet the requirements of a changing society, as proposed by a Nazi regime? It is already possible to modify embryos and even create artificial life,[2] again leading to possible changes to society.

Then, there is always the possibility that, in the future, man might become expendable after machines take over all the heavy lifting, and foot soldiers are no longer required in warfare. Selected specimens of men might then only be required for breeding stock. In such case, women would take over the running of the world along with the machines with men becoming superfluous. The women in turn would then just need to convince the machines that they themselves were still required.

---

[2] China announced cloning of a set of monkey twins in January 2018.

CHAPTER 10

What Will Need to Change

As it is technology bringing in the projected necessity of a universal basic income (UBI), many things will have to change during the transition. Look first at education. In a recent speech,[1] World Bank President Jim Yong Kim spoke about the need for investing in education to prepare for worldwide automation, again recognizing how it was imminent, but without any planned outline on how it should be done. This in part demonstrates how the consequences of the problem are not taken seriously. Certainly, there is a need for better education and to have this aligned with the sort of work that will be available in the future, but not much use when there is no clear definition of what such jobs could be considering advancing AI. The endpoint remains increasing job losses.

It always takes society a long time to catch up with current events, and the educational system is just one of these. Looking back at school syllabuses, a great deal of emphasis was placed on learning facts. It is questionable whether this is in any way still relevant, or why one would need to memorize specific dates of past battles or historical events, when as to facts, everything is available on Google or other search engines. The implication would be that students should be learning how to find, use, and manage those facts and how to advance their thinking, not memorizing facts themselves. The existing concept of teaching to a standard syllabus appears outdated if for no other reason that times change so quickly that, beyond teaching, the basic three Rs, by the time educators decide what is relevant, debate that, legislate, and then introduce the syllabus, it is already out of date.

---

[1] World Bank President, Jim Yong Kim, speaking to an audience at Columbia University in New York, prior to the World Bank's annual meeting in Washington D.C., October 2017.

Career paths will also change. While the one career for life concept has already disappeared, with the advent and speed of new technology in the future, it is likely that people will have not just one, but many jobs during their working life, considering whether they are still even working, and these jobs will not be just in one, but in many disciplines. Consequently, education should be geared toward this changing premise, and even if it is not yet on the horizon, people should be taught how to use their time when they no longer have a job and are simply paid a UBI. How to be unemployed and the required mental adjustment would be a necessary subject on its own. Yet then again, why go to school to study if it is presupposed that later there will be no job? If this is a valid argument, do teachers also lose jobs, and does an AI interface in schools take over all teaching? From high school onward at least, school work requires use of computers, so it is not far removed from these taking over from teachers.

If, however, a UBI would not be enough to keep people with sufficient income for all their desires, perhaps an increase in survival skills training would be necessary. This would involve educating people on how to be able to live on less, how to survive in the wild, or even how to sit in a cave on a mountain and contemplate the relevance of life.

Many things in the way people live will also need to change. Globally, there has been a move from the rural to urban living, and this existing trend will continue. There will be the need for creativity to handle the predicted nine billion people on the planet within 50 years, so housing is likely to be standardized; more apartment style living will be the norm under restricted funding, all of which in turn will require a redesign infrastructure and *greening* of the living space. With this, public transport and movement in general will need to change, where, for example, extensive parking spaces for individual cars will no longer be needed if driverless public vehicles are the norm. There are already *Borrow my car* services where private individuals hire their cars when not in use.[2]

If there is to be a greater emphasis on leisure, this should open a whole new sphere of possibilities from virtual reality situations and interaction with cyborgs. Movies have offered many entries to the future,

---

[2] www.CarNextDoor.com.au

where holidays can be had through virtual reality, rather than visiting a location. It should be possible to select one's companion on the holiday and include any number of add-on options. It might be possible to visit virtual locations on other planets where travel can be at light speed.

Many of these possibilities have yet to be conceived. There is still the need to sort out how this will operate when only some people might still have jobs to earn money, while the rest must operate on a UBI. This will remain one of the major challenges of introducing an inevitable two-tiered society dominated by the majority of UBI *have-nots*. Most importantly, to prevent revolt, the poorer class must be kept interested by affordable options such as by following sport, living in a cyber-world, removing them from (bleak) reality, or side-tracked with freakish amusements as in the movie, *Hunger Games*.[3] Considering the inevitable disparity in incomes of those on a UBI against people who still have other income, the level of acceptance of a UBI system will depend on the amount, which can be afforded to be paid.

---

[3] American dystopian science fiction, 2013.

CHAPTER 11

Funding

Considering that, with the disappearance of jobs and the likely introduction of a UBI, the big question is going to be how to pay for it? Obviously, the money needs to come from government who in turn need to get the money from somewhere. The next question is going to be, if governments are able to provide it, will the money be sufficient?

Government finances constitute revenue and expenditure. A revenue transaction is one that increases the net worth. Revenue is the sum of taxes, net social contributions, sales, other current revenues, and capital transfer revenues. The chief way the government gets the money it spends is through taxation. Annual federal revenues in America are currently around 3.2 trillion U.S. dollars coming from three major sources, income taxes paid by individuals or 47 percent of all tax revenues, payroll taxes paid jointly by workers and employers or 34 percent of all tax revenues, and corporate income taxes paid by businesses representing 11 percent of all tax revenues. The total is 92 percent. There are also a handful of other types of taxes making up the difference, such as customs duties and excise taxes. Customs duties are taxes on imports, paid by the importer, while excise taxes are taxes levied on specific goods, like petrol (gasoline).

The importance of these figures in the UBI concept is that it can be seen how, as an example, 81 percent of the revenue comes from tax on income and payroll. The future UBI funding problem, as easily recognized, is that these figures are based on a current unemployment rate of about 10 percent; so, as jobs disappear and can no longer be taxed, the revenues decrease, while at the same time, UBI (as with any social welfare system), if it exists, becomes another expense item.

As can also be seen, how if corporate income taxes are now only about 11 percent, companies would need to considerably increase their earnings to make up the shortfall in the revenue equation if personal taxes fall. The big question becomes whether the introduction of AI and use of machines and their extra productivity can compensate and achieve the increase of earnings to make up the shortfall, given that if the majority of people are on UBI, their purchasing power will be reduced and so will their tax contributions. In the light of today's technology, it is hard to see how the figures would add up. If the latest annual federal revenues in America are as quoted earlier at around 3.2 trillion U.S. dollars, estimates in 2016 were that, if every person in the United States was paid 10,000 U.S. dollars per annum on a UBI, this would represent a cost of 3.2 trillion U.S. dollars, thereby eating up the total revenue. Were a UBI only applied to people earning under 100,000 U.S. dollars per annum, the calculated cost would be 1.5 trillion U.S. dollars.[1] The two questions that arise are whether individuals would be content with and able to live on 10,000 U.S. dollars a year and how is the arbitrary level at which a UBI commences calculated? At a UBI of 3.2 trillion U.S. dollars, does this lead to national insolvency?

So, the question moves on to whether there can be supplementary earnings from state-owned enterprises (SOEs) to meet the requirements of a UBI no matter what it is, given that SOEs have not been the most efficient in socialist countries[2] because they remove the incentive to work? As demonstrated clearly with farming communes, why work harder if everyone gets the same reward? Could Google, Microsoft, or Amazon work be nationalized to be SOEs to run by governments, and would this be a look into the future? Or, how about taxing these large conglomerates on the specific income they derive by utilizing and selling of the database they collect from users? Looking at a possible future model where most people are paid not to work and presumably factories with robots or AI web-based systems take over, the governments of the various countries could tax these factories (or robots) directly and through indirect measures, utilize these revenues to then distribute UBI to all citizens.[3] Is tax in its various forms

---

[1] Luke Kingma, Futurism, OP.CIT., *https://futurism.com/images/universal-basic-income-answer-automation/*

[2] In Vietnam, for example, SOEs almost crippled the economy.

[3] In the United States, the first tax was in 1861 to fund the Civil War. In Britain, the first taxes were under Roman rule until Lady Godiva had agreed to ride naked through the local town, according to a legend.

to be enough? Would lotteries help keep people with hope while plough-ing back some of the UBI? Perhaps, sources of income not even imagined would emerge considering that taxation as such was possibly invented by the cave man with the biggest club who then had the largest slice of food.

Taxation has continued through the ages in one form or another to satisfy a ruler's requirements, with a large part of this required to fund their wars. The Romans imposed customs duties on the lands they con-quered, and over the centuries, specific taxes have been levied on just about anything from sale of slaves, on sales overall, (GST or VAT), customs duties, payroll, immigration, and salaries. The list is endless. As taxes have never been popular, politicians like to have all these taxes imposed under different names and collected under different agencies so that their overall effect is not too obvious for those who must pay them. Consequently, there are taxes categorized at overall national, state, and local level, as well as indirect taxes on suppliers of people's goods, which are then passed on to the consumer. Will some new possibility and rationale be invented? Meanwhile, humanity must work with what it has.

So, is it then possible to increase the tax rate on the machines or the AI process itself to make up the shortfall in necessary funding? The answer would be that there must be a limit; otherwise, where is the incen-tive to keep the machines working? Without a unified *world order* making decisions, it would always be possible for owners of the means of produc-tion to move to a more favorable tax regime defeating the effect of the tax increase or drop completely off the grid. Would the answer be for some-one to invent a people-less automated type system that just earns money for the government, which could then be distributed? Is it possible to tax *systems,* rather than cash flows?

Adding to the complication of balancing income and expenditure, in most years, the U.S. Federal Government spends more money than it takes in from tax revenues. To make up the difference, the Treasury bor-rows money by issuing bonds, which are bought by institutions such as super funds or by countries. The borrowings are massive. The U.S. debt by 2017 reached 20 trillion U.S. dollars.[4] The Social Security Trust Fund

---

[4] Kimberly Amadeo, *The Balance,* Updated October 26, 2017.

owns most of the national debt, which is in two broad categories, intra-governmental holdings and debt held by the public. Intragovernmental holdings are in turn federal debt owed to 230 other federal agencies. It totals 5.6 trillion U.S. dollars, almost 30 percent of the debt. In August 2017, China owned 1.2 trillion U.S. dollars of U.S. debt or 6 percent as the largest foreign holder of U.S. Treasury securities followed by Japan with 1.1 trillion U.S. dollars. Both Japan and China want to keep the value of the dollar higher than the value of their currencies, so in that way do not act as a direct threat of demanding repayment, but at the same time, there remains an indirect threat when two foreign countries alone hold around 12 percent of another country's foreign debt. A large part of the rest of the U.S. national debt is really pushing paper between government agencies.

Down the road, however, the Treasury must pay back the money it has borrowed with interest. Ultimately, it is difficult to see how such a system can work in perpetuity unless the overall rules are eventually changed. This can always be done if you are the dominant financial country with your currency used as reserve as was achieved when moving from the gold standard,[5] America decided and the rest had to follow. This may not be easy in future, with both China and Russia flexing their international financial muscles. Where the United States runs continuing and mounting deficits, in China, the balance of payment in 2014 recorded a surplus of 257.9 billion U.S. dollars.[6]

So, on the one hand, there is the United States running massive deficits, while China can maintain surpluses and also hold the largest portion of U.S. debt. China does it by running a system where a ruling elite decides what in their opinion is best for the country, their own people, and their communist system to survive. They can manipulate and fix their currency and adjust their trade deals, and the population has been conditioned to accept this rule from the top. It is more difficult to define what, for example, the American system aims for.

---

[5] While paper money was originally backed by gold held, it was manipulated over a long period of time until it could no longer be supported and the Gold Standard was abandoned with other currencies pegged now against U.S. dollars.

[6] China's Balance of Payments Report, 2014.

In attempting an answer, the United States appears to have been founded on the puritanical legacy imported from Britain and is intertwined with capitalism or the concept of private accumulation of wealth. The Frenchman Alexis De Tocqueville in his 1835 *Democracy in America* speculates on democracy's future in the United States. Discussing the possible threats to democracy and possible dangers to the system, he believed that democracy has a tendency to degenerate into *soft despotism*, as well as running the risk of developing a tyranny of the majority, something to speculate on if the majority of people are out of work and have to vote on levels for a UBI. What if that *majority* is the underclass on UBI?

That is the future based on what exists now. The question becomes one of whether it is possible to balance a budget by simply taxing the eventual machines or robotics that will be running everything, or whether some other form of income would be required. On a longer timeframe, how will the accumulated American debt be paid off and where will that money come from because it is unlikely to be as a tax on people receiving UBI? Does the United States just write off the debt when it becomes uncomfortable as was done with the Gold Standard? Would China and Japan simply accept this? It should also not be forgotten that part of the U.S. debt is owed to its own pension fund and the population is aging. Will *money* itself, in the form it is now, continue to exist or to eliminate the problem, would the dollar, Euro, or RMB be moved to some form of cryptocurrency as a standard?

Presumably, these government factories, which in future will have taken over production from humans, will need to be owned by someone, so that will need to be either SOEs, individual wealthy investors, or corporations owned by individuals. If the majority of the population are on a UBI, one would need to wonder whether individuals would then have the money to invest in such factories, and is it questionable whether this leads to a wealthy elite that would emerge to then own all means of production. Or, how well that would be accepted by the remainder? In the past, the global concentration of wealth was not a matter of public record and not easy for all to see, but this has since changed and can be Googled at any time, leaving the public outraged by their findings, learning, for example, that even the Queen of England has holdings in tax havens. Governments can respond where the latter is particularly relevant during current revelations, or how giant corporations can manipulate their tax domiciles to avoid most tax. Yet, tax these giants too highly, and would they still be interested in developing technology, were they not permitted to keep it? All of this is very reminiscent of Ayn Rand's *Atlas Shrugged*. The problem in her conclusion was that, while she speculated that the wealthy could retire to their haven with their technology leaving the bureaucrats to fend for themselves, she did not explain how they would face the problem of isolating themselves from the market and the sale of their products, which made them wealthy.

Looking at the alternatives for funding, there are of course the oil-rich Middle Eastern countries[7] whose revenues proportionate to the population have made many of them rich, both for individuals and in some cases, providing infrastructure, which might be the envy of the world. They can for now afford a high-level UBI. The local population in many cases does not have to strain itself with work; the dirty or unpleasant jobs are passed to immigrant workers, and they keep Filipino maids employed. Qatar, Kuwait, and UAE are the wealthiest,[8] demonstrating that a problem with a UBI for them is, at present, not an issue. On the other hand, one day oil revenues will recede or disappear due to both crude oil depletions and global focus on renewable energy resources. These countries have invested some of their money for the future, but will income from this maintain an oil-driven lifestyle?

The Nordic solution is to simply reduce the days worked. Sweden, in 2018, has introduced a four-day working week on the presumption that workers do more in six hours than in eight and are more relaxed. Some might argue that, if one only gets six hours work out of someone paid for eight, they should only be paid for six. Or, that if the two unproductive hours are people playing around on their mobile phones or on Facebook, removing access to these devices may be a better economic solution. Otherwise, if the same amount of work gets done in six hours, this does

---

[7] The term Middle East focuses on the oil-rich countries in south-west Asia, but overall includes Iran, Iraq, Syria, Kuwait, Saudi Arabia, Bahrain, Qatar, United Arab Emirates (UAE), Oman, and Yemen.

[8] Qatar average income 129,700 U.S. dollars, Kuwait 71,300 U.S. dollars, and UAE 67,700 U.S. dollars.

not mean more employment, but is a worthy thought if an economy can afford to pay for it. In many countries, it would not work.

From the preceding discussion, the Nordic social engineering might be possible with wealthy small populations but returning to the Chinese *Iron rice bowl*, for example, it can be seen that this in the end did not work, even when there was unchallengeable unified control from the top. It would appear that human nature does not, in most cases, want to work for the sake of work, so putting that into the equation, an iron rice bowl is unlikely to work once again. This, except that with the use of AI and robotics those people who do not want to work for the sake of working, would not have to keep the wheels of production going. Perhaps.

These considerations return to the question of whether it will, in future, be possible to develop a financial system where money will be replaced by something people can use to acquire what they need to live on. Presumably, whatever that is, it must be scarce or it does not have value. Picking shells off a beach where they are plentiful is not going to do it. So, what are the alternatives to funding a UBI?

Talking about money creates difficulties because starting with shells, there would not have been enough good ones to go around, so paper money was formed. When that was linked to a gold standard that limited the amount of money, that was okay, but now there is an artificial system linked to mainly the American economy and its dollar as the alternative.

When a bank extends a loan, by banking rules, it is restricted to a lending rate linked to what government regulators force it to hold in reserves. What that means is that banks lend more money than they have to use, which creates national inflationary pressure, meaning they then must keep lending more. Population expansion assists this development, and hence, most governments have to date not want to restrict immigration. It worked for the United States, while the dollar is the main reserve currency.

Meanwhile, the EU has attempted to have the Euro also accepted as a reserve currency on par with the U.S. dollar putting a slight strain on the latter, with China not be far behind in its thinking for the RMB. All of this does not help when there must be increased expansion to pay back the debt created and which would drive the United States into insolvency were all debt to be paid out at once without it printing more money.

Of course, should that ever happen, a new system would need to come into place, but no one has invented that yet. In Switzerland, there is a Bank WIR, which since 1934 has issued its own currency with each WIR equivalent to one Swiss franc, but which cannot be changed for francs with WIR, then becoming simply an accounting system. Again, this may work in Switzerland as a small country, but cannot yet work on a global scale where the banks and governments live on credit. It could, however, provide an example to work on for the future.

Otherwise, following the WIR, credit may be the term of the future and linked to a UBI. Under this, everyone simply receives an allocation of credits or some form of cryptocurrency, which can be held stable against some basket of goods adjusted as consumer price indexes (CPIs) are formulated today. Technically, without inflation, CPIs should remain stationary. The cryptocurrency or credit can be backed by U.S. dollars, Euro, or RMB holdings. Someone, however, still must earn those credits, and populations continue to increase, so this returns to the original problem of how to pay for a UBI and will income from utilization of AI be sufficient.

CHAPTER 12

Legal Framework

The pilot universal basic income (UBI) programs to date work within the existing legal frameworks that would require changes if implemented on a countrywide scale. There are three main issues in bringing in a UBI, the defining of the system to replace other forms of welfare looked at a country-by-country basis, the delivery of the UBI, and then how it is to be financed.

The initial interface in this would be how a UBI connects and replaces social welfare, whether it could be accomplished as a single-step legislation or whether it would be gradual. Looking at the question on a country-by-country basis, in Australia, as an example, there are already areas where three generations have been living on this social welfare. Many unemployed of the employment age are required by law to at least attend interviews for jobs, but most of long-term unemployed (or unemployable) become despondent and simply give up. Their benefits are supposedly curtailed in such instance, but social welfare administrators cannot handle the numbers, and politically, it is not palatable to leave people without income, so the payments continue. One argument for a UBI is that, this would alleviate these constraints by basically facing reality, giving up and just paying. One of the supporting arguments is that these people would be unemployable anyway and have become institutionalized learning to live of the welfare, so are not wanting more. Here is a valuable example of what a future might look like if most people fell into a similar category.

The possibilities of bringing in a UBI looking at the existing trials is to either bring it in stages alongside existing welfare payments or to have it simply replace all welfare payments in one legislative move. The legislative process for a single step itself is not difficult. The argument might be over equality. It might be possible to bring in a UBI at a subsistence level, but then again, is this to be asset-tested, and how would it immediately affect people no longer interested in setting aside savings in their pensions, leaving that to government and would it encourage those on the fringe of the UBI level to give up work as well? Spiraling costs in Australia have seen major rises in numbers spending their superannuation and private hospital insurance to go onto government payments.

America is also experimenting with its health care systems and food stamp systems and has difficulty getting consensus. The problem overall becomes that Band-Aid solutions keep chasing the problem, which is why suggestions supporting a UBI feel this overcomes the problem.

Similarly, from the Chinese example with so many levels of payments spread on a geographical basis, there are the problems of defining needs where expenses are higher in cities than on the farm. Do you allocate as they do now on perceived need, or distribute one UBI that would benefit the farmer more than the city dweller?

Immediately one brings in a UBI for people living on welfare as their only income, delivery becomes important. In Australia, there has been a major problem particularly in indigenous communities where their payments are often used for cigarettes and alcohol bringing other problems with it. Consequently, distribution of the welfare card has been trialed, where this has a restricted use, which cannot be used for buying alcohol. While a logical step, there was immediate criticism from some quarters that this is racial discrimination. In some areas, card holders were found at supermarkets asking other shoppers to give them cash in exchange for use of their cards to buy groceries. Exceptions can most times be found to any rule, but this concept is a start. These issues would not apply were everyone on a UBI card.

No matter how it would be introduced, given the general acceptance of what will happen to a global workforce, the UBI introduction issue needs to be faced. The question becomes the stages in which the system is introduced and how to lessen the disruption during its introduction.

The major issue, of course, in implementation of any UBI will again be how to pay for it, and once more, this raises issues of staged implementation because introduction is unlikely to happen in all countries at once. The overall argument is not about how advanced technology will take jobs, nor really whether this will leave large numbers without work-related income, but more about what governments need to start looking at to address the unemployment issue if they want to retain their current political systems, which for democracy, are funds-driven.

The legislative process around a UBI should be looked at seriously on a countrywide level, focusing on how and when it would logically be introduced and how it will be paid for. When the final decision is made, it is not a difficult legislative process to enact a UBI payment, which supersedes other payments. The question then only remains whether the population considers the payments equitable for people not working, and if not, means tested whether this leads to a dark economy.

CHAPTER 13

What People Do Without Jobs

While it might appear like Utopia to not have to work and yet be paid, assuming always that the system can afford it, the immediate question becomes, what will people do with their unlimited free time? The questions around the subject becomes endless.

Would, in fact, a universal basic income (UBI) remove all incentive to do any work and why would people want to study? A permissible or shadow economy might bring some incentive to still work, but this circumvents the UBI concept and further differentiates between those on limited income (UBI) and those still able to earn on top of it. If there is no incentive to study or work, it must be asked who would be the people designing and running these machines and who would have the training and experience to even run government?

Take the lack of incentives even further and it is possible to visualize everyone with their personal robot looking after their every need. There are already robot vacuum cleaners, window washers, and windows and awnings that open and shut by program, along with stoves that have dinner waiting. Over time, humans will be required to do less and less basic survival work, let alone be assisted in earning an income, and this must influence physical well-being.

So, what do people do with unlimited leisure time? Where it might be a great idea to sit on a beach sipping pinna coladas all day, beaches are limited, parking at the same sites costs money, and exotic drinks do not come cheap?[1] The point in this is that, while it might be great to travel the world and see exotic places, one still requires a certain amount of income

---

[1] Some parking meters (Sydney) automatically photograph cars parking, calculate time parked, and send bills.

or resources to do this, and the question immediately becomes whether a UBI, because of limited resources, will ever be set at a level where people can fulfill their dreams? How will people fund yachts, jet skis, or even robotic vacuum cleaners on a UBI? Will everyone be able to afford to buy and own a personal robot, let alone a home? If not, it would further define a two- or multi-class society.

Some of the arguments for unlimited leisure time have been that this would provide more freedom to stimulate creativity, which might be true to a certain extent. A violinist might be more interested in the music than in what they could earn from it, but it again gets back to how do people pay for the training and who will have the money to attend concerts? Similarly, will painters continue to paint without selling their paintings and will creators of apps continue to do so just for the fun of it, and where will they have received their training?

Then there remain other important issues. Will a UBI and the extra free time encourage people to have more children? Obviously, with lots of free time, it would be possible that more family time might become available, and this is then seen as a good thing. On the other hand, will these children be controllable as they get older? When does a child get their own direct UBI, and what will these children do when they grow up, will they still have needed to go to school, and if so, what sort of subjects will they need to study to lead a productive life? Will governments, as happened in China, decide that the population has grown too rapidly and needs to be curtailed by bringing in a one (or no) child policy? Does one generation on a UBI just lead to subsequent generations also on a UBI?

The same human engineering possibilities would also apply in relation to the aged. Again, quoting the Australian experience mirrored by other countries, the burden on the public purse of the aged is increasing, where pensioners are spending their savings and reverting to what they can get from the government. Should there be a serious financial crisis in funding a UBI, do future governments decide that these old-age people are too much of a burden and carry the currently debated euthanasia laws to their logical conclusion? Looking ahead, it would be possible to see how with a bludgeoning population the aged would be herded together and made so uncomfortable they would be very ready to take a pill without further prompting. Will there be a solution where people found guilty of even minor crimes are executed to reduce the population pressure?[2] It is hard to believe some of this is possible in the future, but it is happening today.

Stretching the imagination, and given that the majority is meant to live on a set UBI, what becomes of the defense forces? Will there be sufficient people, altruistic enough to say, they want to sign up to defend their country and possibly get killed when they could as easily sit on that beach for a livable financial reward? Historically, people joined armies because it was the only job they could get. This is an extreme case, but the same principle applies to many other areas of social service. On the Swiss UBI (defeated) referendum, would someone rather take the 2,500 Swiss franc a month and not risk getting killed even for a little extra? The police would be in a similarly position of would they risk their daily lives for no extra incentive, and if they are paid more, how does the division work between what is meant to be a UBI and jobs that allow people to rise above what will become the ruling class? It is not a good argument suggesting army and police recruits will always raise their hands because they like that sort of authority. Cannon fodder was always there because it had to be, not because people wanted it.

Enno Schmidt, one of the co-initiators of the Swiss UBI initiative and member of the broader Basic Income Earth Network, told the *Irish Times* in February 2016 that "in Europe and the US, democracy is being dismantled and people are deprived of their rights with a growing oligarchy. An unconditional basic income gives democracy a fresh breeze, refreshes human rights and empowers people." He also pointed out that his country's top 1 percent lay claim to over a third of the nation's wealth. The latter comment opens one of the major issues in contemplation of AI future roles because such a wealth percentage is likely to increase under a UBI.[3] In the United States, currently, the richest 1 percent hold about 38 percent of all privately held wealth, while the bottom 90 percent hold 73 percent of all debt.[4] The 1 percent figure is increasing, but how much

---

[2] Online posts show China executing young drug dealers and Philippines law enforcement has killed many drug dealers even outside the legal process.

[3] These percentage figures are wide estimates not accounting for money held in trusts or in offshore arrangements.

[4] *New York Times*, February 2017.

will not be known, given the increasing sophistication of tax schemes.[5] The ultimate tax scheme is where an individual receives the benefit of the money without the constraint of ownership.

These issues point to an eventual move toward at least a two-class system, those on a UBI classified as poor and the rest who can earn some incentive, either from their necessary and remaining job, as investors, or as owners of production. All of this obviously will have some consequence, and it is equally obvious in the society around us today that major fractions are occurring between such class levels. The further implication is that, on the one hand, borders are porous and there is almost a free flow of humanity, while on the other hand, areas within countries become polarized, and now, some areas have become no-go zones. A similar situation has existed in the past in the United States, although a lot of this might have been homegrown racism, whereas in the European countries, this is something fairly new. Evidence is that the original inhabitants are moving more to the country, while the immigrants are taking over the towns.

An influx of immigrants to predominantly Christian-based countries in Europe by other religions has shown that the Christian ethos of *turn the other cheek* only works if others believe in the same thing; otherwise, it is easy to take advantage of it. The Christian concepts are being replaced and the radical un-Christian left pushes the boundaries of conventional thinking with their campaigns for gender fluidity and same-sex marriage, although the latter is basically an oxymoron, given that marriage as it is understood is a religiously defined principle. The question examined here is not about the rights or wrongs of the same-sex debate, but how policy is decided where same-sex legislation in Australia was passed following not a decision of parliament, but after a noncompulsory postal ballot. This could be an indication for future policy, which might be made on other issues outside of democratically elected representatives and a UBI issue becomes contentious.

Many of these new immigrants to Europe are now having to try and get into the welfare system, and the shadow economy is flourishing according to widely reported news. No tax is paid, and yet, the social

---

[5] Including obscure options such as taxes avoided by death at sea. Otherwise, trusts remove ownership details.

welfare benefits flow out for the few who can get them. Having little if any savings from their own countries, standards of living are poor for these people, but then, in many cases, are a lot better than what immigrants left behind. Yet, in these no-go zones, there are areas where people are at liberty in a free speech country to parade in the street shouting that their religion and its followers will take over the country. This is not a religious condemnation, but only to highlight how this right to demonstrate on anything, whether sexual preference or religion has become prevalent, and in many cases, violent. Extend this to a majority population in general with no jobs and time to roam the streets yet still benefiting on a UBI and it becomes difficult to see how authorities will be able to maintain control.

CHAPTER 14

Structural Fluidity

Even with unemployment rising and jobs disappearing, certain parts of the developed world never had it so good in material terms. Generation "Y,"[1] as it is known, have all the opportunities and none of the constraints when one remembers that between 1914 and 1918, the 18-year-olds were off to the trenches, while in 2017, they needed *safe rooms* at schools, in case someone upsets them.

In addition to their having more money than ever before,[2] with marriage breakdowns now fairly common, leaving children with split families, as each parent vies for their necessary time with their kids, these tend to get more spoiled even if more tech savvy. Concurrently, there is more spare time as children spend hours on their electronic devices, whereas before they would have had to play outside or read books. They are the first generation to grow up with complete exposure to current Wi-Fi and Internet technology. They see their parents becoming hooked as well and always on their phones, so it removes the possibility of being trained otherwise. Although kids may get part-time jobs and where would McDonalds be without them, they all have time on their hands and the *progressive* educators do not tie them down to concentrating on the three Rs. Have time on your hands and kids start to explore who they are and what is the purpose of life. Next, they have the opportunity moving into puberty to question their sexuality, and then, from this, have arisen all these invented gender fluidities that cannot be challenged in case it upsets anyone. There are now LGBTQ[3] as variations in sexuality for people

---

[1] Generation Y, Echo Boomers or Millenniums. Born between 1977 and 1994.

[2] In the United States, one in nine Gen Y have credit cards co-signed by parents, WGS Marketing.

[3] Also now extended to LGBTTTQQIAA (Lesbian, Gay, Bisexual, Transgender, Transsexual, Two-spirited, Queer, Questioning, Intersex, Asexual, and Ally with some six other variations within these). The SafeZoneProject.Com

to think about, and such questioning is being introduced into schools. While some children may have been unhappy in their childhood over sexual orientation concerns, it is questionable how many might have been worried about this in the past, and whether it makes them happier to throw further complications into their lives.

With a greater understanding of science in the community, organized Christianity is on the wane with church attendances falling and youth becoming more skeptical at being told that Mary had a virgin birth with which Joseph was okay, and how Jesus is now sitting up on a cloud with God. Certain religions are still fighting the good fight such as the Roman Catholics who provide cheaper schooling if you subscribe, even if you do not believe, while Muslims under Islam are programmed from birth not to question what they are told, are not permitted to disagree, or leave. On the other hand, for the younger people especially, new religious congregations are growing utilizing the lessons people such as Billy Graham taught, with massive feel good events, famous names, and lots of happy clapping in a search for identity. People may have also recognized the historic trend of societies with underclasses uniting around a religion in defense of their treatment with social causes taking on religious overtones.

Where this is relevant within the UBI context relates to what most people with even more time on their hands will want to experiment with? There is now legalized same-sex marriage and not far behind legalized bigamy in Western society whether same sex or not. It leads to other possible combinations in the future not yet invented. It is uncomfortable for some societies to accept that bigamy already exists, and even in countries where this is illegal, a husband can still officially maintain one wife and have other *wives* on the welfare system designated as single mothers. A UBI would simplify this understanding.

While the younger generation has grown up with full exposure to technology, and hence have a good idea of its potential, it becomes a question of whether they will join the race to be part of the future development, or whether at some level, it all becomes bewildering, and they opt out and become unemployed. Already, there is a difficulty in attracting apprentices in the building trades because the prize aim is that university degree, which provides the gate pass to the next step in a career. Going on to academic masters and doctorates, which need to be invigilated by people who have gone the same road before, not wishing to throw disparity on the system, but will this process be fast enough to keep up with cyber development? Will it keep up with AI?

And, what about the fluidity of nationalities between countries where one nationality's response might be different to the dominant nationality in a country. The question relates to the 2017 Australian census, where around 10 percent of the population is now reported as Asian with the major part of that Chinese. Australia has displayed concern about Chinese influence in Australian politics, not to mention that China has bought rights to major ports, infrastructure facilities, and vast farming tracts in the country. At the end of 2017, the Australian parliament introduced a legislation banning foreign donations to political parties, which has increased in recent years. The issue here one needs to consider is whether the Chinese influence will increase in countries outside China, and if it does, do ethnic Chinese rally to support Chinese government policy if called upon to do so?[4] In other words, if China has a dominant position in world politics and pushes for a UBI, will this come in with the support of numbers of the offshore Chinese?[5]

The relevance of these inter-country influences is, in such matters, as the allegations that Russia has interfered with American elections, and there is inference that the Chinese have paid senior politicians in the Australian government to support Chinese policy. None of this is perhaps new, but with the technology today, it is easier to trace. This demonstrates a global political fluidity, which despite race, tends to center in one direction, suggesting the endpoint is a global policy that will not differ greatly between countries. On the other hand, there remains the problem where, for example, China can but land and property in the United States and in Australia, while the same, this does not work in reverse. Chinese back Chinese origins and think in terms of survival of the species (Han) no matter the timeframe. Ethnic Han in this case are around 92 percent of the overall Chinese population with some other 18 minorities. The importance here is that the Han form a very large ethnic group and their decisions in various forms will have a driving influence on future political

---

[4] January 2018, China announced that all people of Chinese origin, no matter where they live, can be granted automatic Chinese citizenship.

[5] Sterling Seagrave, *Lords of the Rim: The Invisible Empire of the Overseas Chinese*, Createspace, March 2010.

policy within China and abroad. They also have a means of controlling large populations while knowing how to contain dissent.

After looking at the fluidity between human ethnic origins toward a possible central order, it is at the same time necessary to look at the fluidity between robots and humans in the decision-making process. Consider first a situation where seniority is built into a specific robot system. Consider if robots are programmed to obey up the line. This is a simple concept, but how then does that one linked system interface with another set of robots that have their own hierarchy programmed in? For example, one set of robots lay tarmac, while another digs up tarmac to lay pipes. From observation, humans have not managed to get that right, so how will programmers be able to put this into robots? To get around the programming problem, you would need *Boss* robots to get the sequence right with the then danger that these could become *superbosses* as AI evolves into self-programming. Could then the superboss controlling all robots below decide it was smarter than humans and take over? Here, there is this ensuing *fluidity* between humans and machines, where on the one hand, the machine is useful, but what is the endpoint when humans rather rely on the machine than another human, and the humans themselves decide, why worry about the human at all and just rely on what the machine decides? The problem of course is that humans can relate to a robot out there to take over, but in the fluidity of AI, the so-called *robot* does not have to be in human form. If made to look like humans, these get the most attention walking, running, and jumping like a human, but the robot can be a box or any other shape and can in fact be online without a physical presence. This means that the *robot* does not even have to be visible form meaning that it is harder to control. This is frightening for humans, but if it were a machine in some human form such as a super soldier, would a soldier rather go into battle protected by a machine which had 10,000 times the capability of identifying and neutralizing threats than the human *mate* alongside? What if that robot stood for election as a war hero having saved many people from attack or calamity, would people vote for it, even if it was only a robot? Does the hero have to be in human form, or as an endpoint, is there fluidity between robots and humans?

CHAPTER 15

Democracy As It Is Understood

The increasing loss of jobs in future is not in dispute, although the extent of the losses and the period may vary, while how this will affect the overall political system of the planet is still unknown.

The job losses issue has had a great deal of attention, but almost nothing has been said about how this will in turn affect the structure of the political system both in individual countries and for the world as a whole. But, change will be required.

Again, the question becomes how much change and whether the democratic systems, as currently understood, will survive. Hawking postulates that they will not, and what will evolve is a singular world government required to control AI.[1] A precursor to such a conclusion is a look at how the earth is now linked through the Internet. There may be separations currently where some governments have their own restrictions as in China, some countries block certain sites and languages differ, but then again, AI has made it possible for anyone speaking in their own language to be understood by someone else in a different language via simple earpieces.

When looking at democracy, it becomes a system of government by the whole population or all the eligible members of the state, typically through elected representatives. Or more loosely defined, control of an organization or group by the majority of its members.

As can be seen from those definitions, the trick revolves around that comment *all eligible members*. These are people able to vote on policy usually pivoted around what is called a *constitution* setting out various rules. In many cases, these constitutions were established by people who did

---

[1] Dom Galeon and Kristin Houser, WIRED Interview, March 14, 2017.

not, in fact, represent the majority in the first place. Under the American system, which is basically a federation of states, there is then an electoral college interposed on top of the system to ensure that individual states, no matter their population numbers, get some proportional say, while in Australia, under its federation, the Constitution allows for direct representation from specified electorates, but then is overseen by a senate intended to be a state house, in which members are elected in equal numbers irrespective of the population. The state of New South Wales on the 2017 census had a population of 7.86 million, while the state of Tasmania's population was only around 520,000, around 6 percent of the larger state yet has the same number of senators. This again suggests that the rules of democracy are really what some people said they are.

The overall system is further regulated downstream by various laws that are enacted by so-called elected representatives and in certain cases, as in the United States, by amendment to the Constitution, which can only be done by special procedures.[2]

Aberrations can result from the process where, for example, in Australia, 20-year olds were eligible for conscription supporting the war in Vietnam, although they did not yet have the right to vote which appeared hardly *democratic*. More seriously, again in an Australian example, the rigid democratic process was circumvented in 2017 through a postal ballot on same-sex marriage where some 79.5 percent of eligible respondents were reported to have said *Yes*.[3] The representative conundrum in this is demonstrated further because nine of the electorates voting No[4] for same-sex marriage were represented by five of the Liberal National Party, which then legislated to bring in the law because this was party policy. If democratic, should elected politicians not be voting according to the wishes of majority of their own electorate that put them there? On the Labor opposition party side, they had a similar problem, when they were not yet in power. This unofficial voting was also at a time when the legality of the parliament was itself under question after many sitting members of both

---

[2] Three-quarters of the states must affirm the proposed Amendment or a Constitutional Convention to be called by two-thirds of the legislatures of the states.

[3] Results released by government statistician 10 a.m. EST November 15, 2017.

[4] Electorates had large Muslim populations.

houses were discovered to be ineligible to sit or even be elected because of their dual nationality.[5] These issues demonstrate how the democratic process can breakdown, and in the latter example, raises the legality of any legislation that was earlier passed by these members not duly elected.

Where the senate as in Australia is meant to be a house of review looking after state rights, it has become a party-backed institution, rather than looking after local interests. In America, as during the election of Donald Trump to President, whether rightly or wrongly, it still raises the question of how you can win an election and run a country without having the majority of votes, and does this express the will of the majority of people? In fact, it goes back to the definition of democracy.

Additionally, under democracy, there are the rules that are established governing the voting procedure itself where it is possible to have proportional voting with preferences, or alternatively election on *first past the post*. The effect of some of these rules on how democracy will work then result in the person put into power having less than 50 percent of the primary vote. For example, with 20 nominations for a position, it would be possible for someone on *first past the post* to have say only 15 percent of votes and still become elected. Alternatively, on proportional voting, the idea is that the elected person gets some benefit from people who do not vote for them as a first preference, so the candidate does not win as a first choice, but is elected on a consensus. Again, this depends on the rules one uses for the definition of democracy. Each method attempted to make the process truly *democratic* or fair, but that does not always please everybody. Is any of this really democratic process, or what in fact is true democracy?

Under *participatory democracy* as introduced by the Australia Party, which at one time controlled government through the upper house in Australia, there were elected representatives, but the nominations were carried out through postal vote available to all members. Similarly, starting with a policy, which was initially written by the founder, IPEC mogul, Gordon Barton, each section was later revised and voted on by postal ballot.[6] While it would seem this sort of system would be fairer than what currently applies, it is far more difficult to operate continual

---

[5] Article 44 of Australian Constitution.

[6] Author was on first National Executive and National Returning officer.

ballots than party room meetings and can be manipulated by interested parties or taken over by fringe groups. Extend the *participatory* principle to the AI age and one could envisage a system where all registered voters had an online app where firstly, as under the Swiss system, people could call for a referendum, and if accepted, voters hit their response button for instant legislation on the will of the majority. Want to increase the UBI? Bing: and it is done.

Democracy, as it was intended, can be put under an unfavorable microscope on many occasions, and it is really an enigma when one has a *truth in advertising* law, but this does not apply to political comment or political parties outside of the parliament. Similarly, it is questionable when parties can be represented in parliament through well-known celebrities and elected although the parties they represent contain few members.[7]

Regarding democracy, in general, in most countries across the globe, only a few places, such as Britain, the United States, and as far away as New Zealand, have enjoyed an unbroken parliamentary system for more than a century. The country that shines on the democracy scale is Switzerland with only seven million people and almost 3,000 autonomous municipalities, 26 sovereign states and a federal level. Most laws are decided by the parliament, not by *indirect* democracy as in Britain, and Swiss citizens are entitled to forward any law decided by their representatives to a general vote. To do this, they just need to gather 50,000 signatures calling for a change within 100 days of posting a new law, a number that is approximately 1 percent of the electorate. In 96 out of 100 cases, no such referendum has been triggered because lawmakers are careful in how they pass the laws in the first place, but at least, the options for reversal are there.[8] All citizens are also able to propose any constitutional amendments they wish, provided they do not go against international law or human rights. For this to happen, they need to gather a minimum of 100,000 signatures within 18 months. Testing this procedure and how it would affect a UBI, it must be remembered that Switzerland on June

---

[7] The Australia Party when holding power in Australia via the senate had around 700 members.

[8] Bruno Kaufman, President of IRI Europe, a Brussels-based think-tank.

05, 2016, put a UBI to a referendum that was defeated. Although the official text for the vote did not specify the level of a UBI, the campaigners proposed 2,500 Swiss francs (around 2,500 U.S. dollars) per month for adults and 625 francs for children. No one will really know whether the defeat was on principle or because of amount. However, under what might otherwise seem a fairly egalitarian political system, which might overcome the possibility of voters clambering for excessive payments, it, at the same time, opens the possibility that, despite what governments or elected representatives might want, the Swiss system would allow citizens to vote for a higher UBI despite what legislator's decree. Consequently, the overall government system would be at the mercy of the voters, irrespective of the ability to pay.

Looking more closely at what constitutes democracy, it is not always a very clear-cut procedure and often does not pass the *one person one vote* test, remembering that, in America, voting is not compulsory. The idea under this system is that only people interested should decide policy anyway, but this leads to special interest groups pushing their policy through. In Australia, voting is compulsory, but is it fairer to get people to vote on issues they do not care about or for people they do not know? When having to decide which system is fair, the Swiss or on what is called the Nordic system, is probably as near as it is possible to get to something *fair*, remembering, however, that, when referring to small cohesive populations in these countries at that level government, it is easier to control.

Looking closely at what the Western concept of democracy involves, it is seen to include capitalism as one of its elements. So, *ownership* becomes a large part of democracy in various forms where it has been long argued that the Scandinavian, Nordic overall welfare system is a shining example of looking after its citizens. In the Scandinavian countries, like all other developed nations, the means of production are primarily owned by private individuals, not the community or the government, and resources are allocated to their respective uses by the market, not government or community planning. Within this, Scandinavian countries provide a generous social safety net and universal health care, yet it is argued this not being the same thing as socialism or capitalism, but social democracy. In such a system, the government aims to promote public welfare through heavy taxation and spending, within the framework of a capitalist economy. In talking about Nordic countries such as Norway, Denmark, and Sweden, it must be remembered that Norway benefits from massive income from its oil, making it easier to fund any welfare.

Otherwise, in these Nordic countries, there is no set minimum wage, and these are decided by collective bargaining agreements between unions and employers. This system, as elsewhere, locks out the least skilled and is not aligned with a UBI principle. Scandinavia has been able to introduce its systems being largely a region based on family-driven agriculture. The result is a nation of small entrepreneurial enterprises directed by citizens facing the same set of challenges. Solutions that benefit one member of the society are likely to benefit all members, resulting in a collective mentality that trust its government because the government is led by citizens seeking to benefit everyone. Accordingly, they are willing to go along with paying higher taxes in exchange for benefits that they get to enjoy such as funded health care and education, which are of such high quality that a private enterprise has no reason to offer them. This mindset remained intact as capitalist enterprises developed.[9]

As with everything, there is a down side. For the Nordic model, these dangers come from immigration and an aging population, while at the same time, the rate of economic development or gross domestic product is not as high as in other advanced economies limiting growth. Scandinavia attracts a notable influx of newcomers seeking to enjoy the generous public benefits. These new arrivals often come from nations that do not have a long, shared history of making decisions on behalf of the common good and bring their divisive cultural agendas with them. While native Scandinavians tend to have a high degree of participation in the workforce as part of their collective decision to support the amenities their society offers, immigrants do not always share this vision. These new arrivals are a major economic burden to the system and hold it in jeopardy by weight of numbers, who if they stay, will be able to vote. The Nordic model redistributes assets, limits the amount of money available for personal spending and consumption, and encourages reliance on government-subsidized programs. In voting, the immigrants might not

---

[9] The Nordic Model: Pros and Cons, Investopedia https://investopedia.com/articles/investing/100714/nordic-model-pros-and-cons.asp#ixzz53Orx836

appreciate those restrictions and would be able to decide on increases in benefits, which a balanced, low-level economic level might not be able to afford.

Having determined that democracy is what the *free world* is aspiring to by one definition or another, the question is how this responds to a changing world and whether the system can withstand the rapidity and intrusiveness of artificial intelligence where the vast majority of humans are without a job?

CHAPTER 16

The Other Side of Democracy

Looking at historical major changes in the political structure, while needing to use a broad brush, it can be seen how over time, countries were subject to major changes in their fortunes. From the advanced civilization of the ancient Egyptians where dynasties lasted for centuries to disappear apparently through administrative squabbling, certain lessons can be learned. The whole Inca civilization virtually disappeared and archeologists speculate on what happened to Angkor Watt before it became reclaimed by jungle.

In more recent times, it is possible to look at factors leading up to American, Russian, and French revolutions, which turned whole countries inside out to be eclipsed by Mao's communist cementing the overthrow of the war lords, then resulting in the deaths of millions.

America

Using a broad brush over history, the American Revolution between 1765 and 1783 was instigated when the ruling British government decided to make the American colonies pay a large share of their French and Indian War debt. Through the Sugar Act, Stamp Act, and other taxes, such as on tea (Boston Tea Party), the British tried to collect taxes the American people considered harsh. The call was *No taxation without representation*. The American Revolution was in essence a colonial revolt during which the *American patriots* in 13 colonies defeated the British backed by France. The history of this is well known and is taught in all American schools.

In analyzing the contributing factors to the change in power, it can be seen:

- Large number of *colonial* class people
- Feeling unrepresented: *No taxation without representation*
- Oppression from ruling classes, the British (and French)
- Political move against ruling (British) class leading to a new form of government
- Had own military support (colonials all had guns; see second amendment)[1]

France

The French Revolution began in 1789 and ended in the late 1790s with the ascent of Napoleon Bonaparte. During this period, French citizens destroyed much of its past political and cultural landscape. Like the American Revolution before it, the French Revolution was influenced by enlightenment ideals, particularly the concepts of popular sovereignty and inalienable rights. Although it failed to achieve all its goals, and at times, degenerated into a chaotic bloodbath, the movement played a critical role in shaping the modern nation by showing the world the inherent power of the (poorer) people. Over 17,000 people were officially tried and executed during the Reign of Terror, and an unknown number of others died in prison without trial.

In 1795, the National Convention, composed largely of Girondins, who had survived the executions, approved a new constitution that created France's first bicameral legislature. Executive power was enshrined in the hands of a five-member *Directoire* appointed by the parliament. Royalists and Jacobins protested the new regime, but were swiftly silenced by the army led by Napoleon Bonaparte.

It is well known that Napoleon was eventually defeated having dominated Europe between 1800 and 1814, after which the rulers of Europe wanted to ensure that such a revolution would not occur again, particularly for Louis XVIII, whose brother Louis XVI had been executed during the revolution. He granted amnesties, but the wealthy, remembering the leveling effects of the revolution, became passionately anti-revolutionary. The French political system has evolved since 1789, with the two world

---

[1] Part of American argument for right to own guns under the Second Amendment.

wars having a major impact. The current form of the French system dates from 1958 to today's Fifth Republic, which came about following a political crisis over France's colonial war in Algeria, when Charles de Gaulle took power under a new constitution that gave the president new executive powers, making the post uniquely powerful in European politics. The power of De Gaulle can be seen as a legacy of his involvement after the overthrow of Germany after France had been a part of Germany.

In analyzing the contributing factors to the change in power, it can be seen:

- Large number of poor peasant class people
- Feeling unrepresented
- Oppression from ruling classes
- Political move against ruling class
- Had military support

Russia

Proceeding then with the broad brush to the Russian experience, the Russian Revolution of 1917 involved the collapse of an empire under Czar Nicholas II and the rise of Marxist socialism under Lenin and his Bolsheviks. Its effect was felt around the world.

Much of Western Europe viewed Russia at the time as an undeveloped, backward society practicing serfdom with landless peasants forced to serve the land-owning nobility. In 1861,[2] the Russian Empire finally abolished serfdom, but its effect lingered because the *serfs* had no chance to accumulate capital and festered continued resentment. The mystical religious presence of Rasputin[3] in the Czarina's ear had stirred the aspirations of the poor, so nobles eager to end Rasputin's influence murdered him on December 30, 1916. By then, most Russians had lost faith in the failed leadership of the Czar. Government corruption was rampant

---

[2] Russia was still on the Julian calendar, so references show 25 October as date.
[3] Grigori Rasputin, the *Mad Monk* was an outlandish figure in the court of Czar Nicholas II of Russia accepted after supposedly curing the Czar's son Alexis of hemophilia.

and the Russian economy remained backward. While two wars involving Russians did not help and a major famine played a part, the Romanoffs lost control. The autocratic rule of the Czar among a majority peasant population had him forced to put up a political front in formation of a Duma supposedly ruling the country while he ignored its decisions when it suited him.

Demonstrators with large crowds of striking workers clashing with police and when they would not disperse, the army was called in and fired into the crowds killing some but the protesters continued. A few days later Czar Nicholas abdicated the throne, ending centuries of Russian Romanov rule.[4]

The Civil War broke out in Russia in late 1917 after the revolution between the factions included the Red and White Armies, where the Red Army fought for the Lenin's Bolshevik government and the White Army represented a large group of loosely allied forces, including monarchists, capitalists, and supporters of democratic socialism. The Civil War ended in 1923 with Lenin's Red Army claiming victory and establishing the Soviet Union.

In analyzing the contributing factors to the change in power, it can be seen:

- Existence of a large poor ex-serf class
- Disenchanted workers
- No representation within government
- Oppression from rulers (wealthy ruling class)
- Political move against ruling class
- Eventual armed conflict to establish and cement a political system.

China

Looking at the Chinese Great Proletarian Cultural Revolution, it was a decade-long period of political and social chaos caused by Mao Zedong's bid to use the Chinese masses to reassert his control over the Communist

---

[4] Anna M. Cienciala, University of Kansas, *The Russian Revolutions of 1917.*

party. His revolution was launched in May 1966, but his wide-sweeping political intervention leading to the death of millions was in effect 17 years after his troops seized power. The struggle had been, as released in one of his early statements, "To struggle against and crush those persons in authority who are taking the capitalist road ... so as to facilitate the consolidation and development of the socialist system."[5]

Before the Chinese Communists came into power, China was an underdeveloped country, which for centuries had been divided between numerous warlords, tribes, and hereditary landlord dynasties that fought among each other for power and wealth. The average lifespan of a Chinese person was to their mid-40s (to over 70 post Mao), and hospitals were a luxury mostly reserved for the wealthy. Illiteracy was common, and remote tribes practiced slavery where women were bought and sold as a matter of course[6] being one of the reasons for their importance in Mao's promoting communism, which treated them as (almost) equals.

War lords had their own armies and continually formed alliances, which continued when military and political leader Chiang Kai-shek joined the Chinese Nationalist Party (known as the Kuomintang, or KMT) in 1918 (coinciding with the end of the 1914–1918 First World War), and succeeded party founder Sun Yat-sen as KMT leader in 1925. Despite a professed focus on reform, Chiang's government concentrated on battling Communism within China, as well as confronting Japanese aggression where the Allies declared war on Japan in 1941. The Civil War broke out with the communists in 1946 (a year after end of the Second World War), bringing in an eventual victory by Mao Zedong's Communist forces and the creation of the People's Republic of China.[7] Chiang led the KMT government in exile in Taiwan with major support from the Americans.

Again, encapsulating another revolution, it is possible to look at the main contributing factors arising from the different aspects of life before the revolutionary Civil War to see whether any lessons can be learned.

---

[5] Columbia University, *Asia for Educators*, http://afe.easia.columbia.edu

[6] Called mui-tsai or *Little sisters*.

[7] Jung Chang's *Wild Swans*, Harper Press latest 2012, provides graphical description of transition from feudalism, through Mao to the present day.

- Existence of a large poor uneducated worker class
- Disenchanted workers, particularly women who were treated very badly
- No representation within (or understanding of) government
- Oppression from rulers (wealthy ruling class)
- Political move against ruling class
- Ongoing small scale then eventual armed conflict to establish and cement political system.

Second World War

Then there was also the Second World War,[8] which while not actually a revolution and not a Third Reich success, had similarities (and timing) to the other major changes in the political landscape. It showed the similarity in having a German and then Japanese population, which backed their leader's revolt after the people felt they had become marginalized. Hitler capitalized on this *underdog* theme and how the poor Germans had been treated following the First World War. While the population may not have been totally impoverished, their national identity they felt had been slighted. Hitler used the Jews as his enemy symbolic of a wealthy upper class to give the population a target to aim for.

Overall

Looking then at the contributing factors from these revolutions in America, France, Russia, and China, it is informative that they all contain similar components. The question becomes whether any of these conditions show signs of surfacing today and whether job losses leading to an eventual (a) poor underclass of people on a UBI, who are then (b) disenchanted (c) feel they have no representation (d) are oppressed by their ruling class of elite (wealthy billionaire leaders), whether this would lead toward eventual uprising to change the political system, and

---

[8] For Europeans, the Second World War began in 1939 when Germany invaded Poland. For Americans, it began in December 1941. The war in Europe ended in May 1945 and in August 1945 in the Pacific.

- the big question then of whether the system in place would permit them to succeed, or not, and
- whether transition would be accompanied by violence and revolution?

The overall question becomes whether the social change instigated by revolt of an underclass, which felt unrepresented, provided the revolutionaries with better representation, or whether it eventually led back to a ruling class, either under a democratic, socialist, or communist system? Do political agendas go around in circles, and will a UBI eventually cement consistency?

CHAPTER 17

Evolving Political Framework

Two recent major shocks to accepted global expectations have been the election of Donald Trump coming from outside the ruling political class as the American President and BREXIT, neither of which was expected by the global media.[1] While a great deal of analysis has followed both decisions, it appears clear that voters had become disillusioned with the political process and were prepared to *shoot themselves in the foot* just to have a change. The larger the sample, the greater chance for variance. In Trump's case, there was the added benefit for the novelty available to the media circus, and in BREXIT, this could perhaps be explained by anyone who has ever dealt with departments within the EU in Brussels and found the intransigence of having to deal with the multiple levels of bureaucracy.[2] In both cases, the impact of social media on the results demonstrated its effect and relevance, particularly in relation to timing. Politicians were able to circulate messages to a wide audience and have this timed, so that the opposition did not have a chance for reply.

It also introduced the coining of *fake news*, which had been around for some time, but never achieved the same focus, where now other countries such as Russia could be accused of interference in American (and later British) elections. Then, there was WikiLeaks releasing documents the government never wanted anyone to see and the 11.5 million leaked *Panama papers*, making public that world leaders are involved in financial

---

[1] Both were predicted with explanation by the author long before Trump had won the nomination.

[2] Dealing with legal issues, it is necessary to go through the EU under their legislation who then pass this on to the national legislation, which then can be bogged down if there is any difference between the two.

practices their constituent would frown upon. Of course, aligned with the fake news concept is the question of *fake trust*.[3] This can run from trusting your bank to trusting thousands of companies to which you give credit card details to. Some companies, once they have your details, continue to charge for dubious services, and it is then almost impossible to contact them to obtain a refund.

The amount of data now available globally is making it impossible to digest everything relevant to a particular subject, and so computers are used to sift and highlight specifics. That in itself creates problems, where, for example, Googling the siege in the Iranian embassy in 1980 gives you an entirely different slant on facts than when going through a more sympathetic localized search engine. In other words, many facts are out there, but not all are accurate. Overall, it is proving that the world is getting smaller, with some institutions having a little difficulty catching up on accuracy.

Getting back to specifics and the consequence of the democratic principle of enshrined "government by the whole population or all the eligible members," going to the Australian situation, there is a welfare system, including a Medicare system that is costing the country billions. For politicians to try and reduce benefits would lose them government, and individual members can lose their seats. A recent election was lost when the Labor party ran a scare campaign on the eve of the election that the Liberal coalition would introduce a small fee for a visit to a doctor.[4] This was run not by a party, but by an aligned group *Get Up* on the same *Tea Party* principle and gave no time for the other side to respond before voting. The same last-minute attacks were aimed at Hilary Clinton in the last American presidential campaign, giving her insufficient opportunity to respond.

Still, in Australia, in relation to its Medicare system, GP attendance, which is bulk billed, in 2016–2017 had patients access 148.8 million

---

[3] Rachel Botsman, *Who Can You Trust? How Technology Brought Us Together—and Why It Could Drive Us Apart*, Public Affairs. University of Oxford's Saïd Business School, November 14, 2017.

[4] Federal election 2010, leading to hung parliament, but swung to labor on a coalition agreement.

Australian dollars at a cost of 7.5 billion Australian dollars, an increase of 2.7 percent on the previous year.[5] To this needs to be added hospital and pharmaceutical benefits that are also covered. Social security and welfare payments represent 35 percent of the Australian government's expenses. The level and sustainability of this expenditure has been a key budget issue, especially since the introduction of a new National Disability Insurance Scheme and assistance to the aged.[6] In 2016–2017, the Australian government calculated that it will spend around 158.6 billion Australian dollars on social security and welfare rising to around 191.8 billion Australian dollars in 2019–2020.[7] This category of expenditure includes a broad range of payments and services.[8] The cost of welfare often focuses only on cash payments to working age people such as unemployment benefits and the Disability Support Pension (DSP), but these payments only represent around 17 percent of welfare expenditure (around half) as presented in the budget and are not the main drivers of growth in expenditure. In total, there are around five million people receiving direct individual income support out of a total population of around 24 million, or 20 percent of the population. The figures can be presented in many ways by politicians, but in response to the Australian Liberal Democrat Senator David Leyonhjelm calling for a reduction in government spending,[9] the fact-checking system[10] confirmed that the proportion of Australian adults receiving cash payments was below 50 percent, but that, at least 50 percent of Australian households receive government payments.[11] Within a broad framework as to accuracy, these figures demonstrate that a large

---

[5] Australian government Department of Health and Ageing, 2016–2017 figures.

[6] Michael Klapdor and Don Arthur, 2016, Australian Government Library, *Welfare, what does it cost?*

[7] Australian Government Estimates, 2016–2017, Statement 5.

[8] Including most income support payments such as pensions and allowances, family payments such as Family Tax Benefit, paid parental leave pay, child care fee assistance payments, funding for aged care services, funding for disability services, and payments and services for veterans and their dependents.

[9] Australian Broadcasting Commission ABC News Radio Breakfast, April 30, 2015.

[10] ABC, op.cit, Fact checking of news system, http://abc.net.au/news/factcheck/

[11] FactCheck, op.cit, May 11, 2015.

proportion of the country's population can now be dependent on government handouts, and this is still within a situation where statistics record only around 5 percent unemployment. The awakening must come when one considers that if half the population is already supported in one way or the other by the government in Australia, what would be the implication of that unemployment rate rising steeply or even climbing to a predicted 60 or 80 percent?

As mentioned earlier, quoting the Australian example, there have already been casualties in politicians losing their seats if they do not respond to the wishes of the electorate, which may be all very well if some worthy cause was involved, such as in voting for pollution reduced or regarding improving safety on the roads, but this would be a different story were a politician or a political party to interfere with the welfare payments people have become accustomed to. Logically, the voters would not like this very much. Take that one step further and hypothesize that the same governments must fix the annual level of a UBI at a time when the then majority of the voting population has become dependent on it. The party or individual politician who offers a higher rate is likely to be the one elected, and there will always be those outside of the mainstream parties who will want to gain publicity by supporting public causes such as increased UBI. It would be extremely difficult for a political party to reduce a UBI rate once introduced even if there were funding difficulties. See similarities with *Obamacare* and how difficult it has been to roll back a cause once legislated.

Elaborating on this hypothesis further, a scenario is likely where politicians scramble to offer more and more UBI until ultimately the system would collapse for lack of funds.

In the Trump case, he managed to win a presidential race because, as with AI development, he did not sit within the conventional box, offering a guide to what might happen in the future. Who would have believed there would ever be a president tweeting his general opinions to the public at large 24/7 at a time when an earlier big blown up issue had been whether Hilary Clinton had used her private mobile phone? This might only be a small example of change in what the public see as normal, but is significant as an indication of how politics will be run in future, from suggested WikiLeaks revelations to Russian influence in deciding election outcomes, or as with the voter scare on Medicare in Australia, having fake news sent out to voters on the eve of an election, leaving no time for reply.

Looking at BREXIT, which at the end of 2017, appears to be moving toward some level of agreement, reports filtering through on the Australian media[12] in December 2017 have suggested that the whole decision is visibly polarizing opinion in the United Kingdom with the older generation resistant to change, while the youth of the day is not worried about the consequences of what change might bring.

---

[12] Steve Price, Macquarie Media, December 08, 2017.

CHAPTER 18

Adjusting to Change

Possibly, the biggest hurdle humanity has today is to come to terms with and handling the prospect of change. The Western literature is still predominantly focused on development in Europe. Here people knew their place and it did not matter whether you were a shoe maker or baker as long as you made good shoes and baked good bread. The local squire was accepted, and nobility, even now, is revered for little other reason than because it is there. Traditions followed through generations. Europe developed on a very class-conscious society.

Then along comes the global population movement and things are not, and are unlikely to ever, be the same again. The most common name in the English phone books is now reputed to be Patel and not Smith. Society has never really liked change as it can make people uncomfortable, and consequently, it is far easier to accept the *status quo* and to believe that future change will just affect other people and life will go on more or less as it always has. But, change will come.

Adding the components of change to those facts of which one can be certain, the question arises about how this adjustment will be achieved?

Reduced to its simplest form, if a universal basic income (UBI) is required, governments under a one person one vote (democratic) system will not be able to pay an ever-increasing higher rate for a UBI or an equivalent welfare payment just because electors want (or need) it. The benefit must be supportable from revenue (income). If people do not have jobs and are not working, it is then not possible to directly tax them. On the other hand, trying to keep a UBI static without regular increases would be difficult, so it is likely that a UBI would contain an institutionalized cost of living index to save the politicians becoming involved. At the same time, it would be political suicide once established for politicians to reduce it. So, where does a political system go from there?

The first reaction of most governments to handle such problems has always been to establish an *independent commission*; in this case, to set the UBI rates absolving themselves of the consequences of having to make decisions. That can work when there are still few people under a UBI, but the difficulty increases as a larger proportion of the population must also join. Here, remember that somehow the system still must find the money to pay.

And, here is the crunch. As there will still need to be some people to keep the world running, these people will have to receive some incentive payment above a UBI. Owners of AI systems and factories required to keep things going will also need to be able to retain their incentives. Owners of intellectual property must be able to retain it, and they are unlikely to go along with the type of Directive 10-289 in *Atlas Shrugged* forcing everyone to handover their patents to the government. Against these owners of wealth, you have the large portion of the global population simply sitting on a UBI with a massive income divide. It must result in a two-tiered society, and it can be seen what occurred when this happened in the past. Remember now that all those UBI recipients will have ample time in which to create mischief if they wish, and there will be very many of them. Anyone just has to think back to the French Revolution or what happened to the Russian aristocracy? The signs were there in both instances, but those comfortable at the top refused to see them.

Because obviously, change in the political system, even through revolution, will not come in all countries; at the same time, there will be, as seen already, migration toward countries that have a generous welfare system away from countries where there are few jobs and no social security. Countries reacting to this must attempt stricter border controls or try and accommodate the influx of economic refugees within their economies. How do politicians react? They have a dilemma where, on the one hand, they must be seen as hard and support an anti-immigration policy for their traditional constituents, while on the other hand, not losing votes from (large) numbers of newcomers. In democratic systems, which see themselves as benevolent, politicians first try and take a harsh stance on immigration as in Australia,[1] whereas, in a Socialist, Communist, or Arab

---

[1] Stop the boats policy intercepting boat arrivals and relocating them off shore.

systems, it is easy for the leaders to simply rule that no one is let in.[2] In still *democratic* although less altruistic regimes, leaders can still rule who they will let into their country as in Japan, where they even specify that no one of a specific religion can be allowed to become a citizen.

In trying to tighten border control, it is also necessary to limit the extent of social benefits paid out to residents, even if not citizens. Once people are in the country, it would be unacceptable for part of the (citizen) population to be on a UBI, while hoards of the remaining numbers have no income and must rely on the dark economy, the drug trade or worse.

Back to who will make these political choices? As implied under democracy, there is an increasing pressure toward the *nanny state* with increasingly controls on the population, but coupled with the need for politicians to react. In the West, if someone has their toe stuck in a bath tub, some politician will make a speech on how this is a threat to humanity and immediately legislation is enacted to govern the size of plug holes. All of this might be commendable and certainly gives the minister in charge of bath tubs a moment in the limelight, but the reality from Economics 101 is that, ultimately, people will respond to money available to them, with which they decide where this should go, whether on food, schooling, entertainment, or for capital accumulation, the cornerstone of capitalism.

So, there is the dichotomy in a capitalistic society in bringing in a UBI for people who just cannot find a job and those who can have incentive payments above a UBI just to ensure that the wheels of the world keep turning.

The problem then returns to when creating this two-class global society, with the estimated up to 80 percent on a UBI in the poorer class who have presumably little surplus income with which to invest, but have lots of free time; is this majority going to accept the situation or will they revolt?

How does this work then in a heavily planned top-down form of government? In looking at China, it is a mistake to take the 2,924 hands raised in by the National People's Congress in the Great Hall of the People

---

[2] Arab countries such as Saudi Arabia will not accept Muslim refugees from Syria, Japan will not permit Muslim immigrants, and China or Vietnam do not have alien citizenship.

approving a resolution as simply dictatorial. In fact, many quite-heated discussions do take place regarding policy issues before they are decided, but culturally, once an issue is finalized, everyone gets behind it. Having said that, it is still a very top-down system, particularly when it comes to security of the party and different people's votes have different values. It is a system such as in Africa where the chief listens to all opinions of his advisors and then decides what is best. Hopefully, that is not restricted to what is just best for him. By contrast, a standard reaction in many African countries when raising the subject of a Westminster Democratic system is, "Who ever heard of an Opposition Chief?"[3]

The point in *democracy* is about how those people making the decisions are selected. That is why, there is an *opposition,* which in the words of Don Chipp, the founder of the Australian Democrats in 1977, was there to *Keep the bastards honest.*[4] Under the Chinese system, you must be in the party and accept established party policy to be elected, after which you can add comments from the bottom, but then again, this becomes heavy top-down. Such a system of course can theoretically handle a UBI. In China, after Mao, with all means of production in government hands, people have few alternatives. Over time, as can be seen, the *commune* concept falls apart at the seams with China, now allowing individual private enterprise leading to creation of many billionaires. On the other hand, the wealthy elite all appear to maintain close links with a government practicing communism, while the masses know their place. Historically, this has always been the same because the politicians need the moneyed people to keep them in power so they in turn look firstly after the interests of the moneyed. In China, there remains the strong control from an elite at the top.

The enigma here is that, while China and its form of government comes across as being an option for how a UBI could run, given that all of its government employees are already on the *payroll* even after the end of the *iron rice bowl,* and China can afford to aim for space stations and trips to Mars, they also show all the indicators or heading to an increasingly

---

[3] From author's extensive experience in most African countries.

[4] Australia's largest minor party from formation in 1977 through to 2004 and frequently held the balance of power in the senate during that time.

two-tiered population that might not always go along with this. The reason technology is accelerating such an outcome is because of communications within which it is hard to hide disparities in lifestyles. North Korea tries to shut its population away from reality, but with new technology, films and news from the outside world slip in.

All of the aforementioned indicates that change is coming and it is all about whether it comes gradually or with a *big bang*. The latter of course referring to what would change with something like an all-out war with North Korea. At present, China can keep them in check with North Korea dependent on them for oil and many essential commodities, but when dealing with someone such as Mao, the world has found how many people could be sacrificed for a leader's self-aggrandizement. Third World War remains a reality. With all this, there will be a greater reliance on machines, and as has been seen in past engagements, some of the world's major technological advancements have been introduced in response to war. The bomb took Japan out of the Second World War, and perhaps, a new all-out war might further enhance the advance of the machine.

All the indicators point in some similar direction where, as Stephen Hawking has already postulated, this leads to a logical outcome when machines come into dominance. The question remains whether this, as he also suggests, leads to a singular world government, which can then control AI or whether man loses the contest?[5]

---

[5] WIRED interview, Dom Galeon, Kristin Houser, March 14, 2017.

CHAPTER 19

Military Intervention

AI in context of the military and possible armed conflict needs to be considered in relation to actions between countries, within countries, and then between man and machines. Science fiction books and movies have depicted the progression of what might happen after the machines decide they no longer need human intervention.

In global conflicts to date, the technological advance has been largely one sided with, for example, one country dominating airspace, although that did not secure a win for Russia in Afghanistan nor for the United States in Vietnam. In those cases, sheer numbers of people and leaders prepared to sacrifice lives, no matter what the cost overcame the technology. The point illustrated here is the possibility of future generations with masses of unemployed employing the same concept. Should, however, computer-driven robot armies be the way of the future, robot armies killing each other as in a Star Wars movie would degenerate to who, in the end, had the most robots. Would a complete robot army have a single *kill switch* one could go after? More frightening would be were none such available and a war once started would be out of human hands and not be stopped.

In military conflict between countries, AI will, in the end, be decisive in building own capacity to strike, while at the same time, attempting to disable the technology of the other side. In a global economy, the distinction of national borders and country on country conflict becomes gray. While in past conflicts, there have always been fifth columns within a country, with the rise of acts of terrorism, this raises the threat from within. This remains a complex subject on its own where concern here is how this will affect the number of jobs. While provision of security is a growth industry, it is largely assisted by nonhuman systems providing such things as face recognition technology and CCTV applications blanketing some areas.

Looking at the overall military position, there is one side utilizing AI to attack, while the other AI is designed for defense. Where the problem starts is when humans then need to build automatic systems to respond to threats and build *survival* modules into their programming. In essence, this ultimately locks out human intervention and allows the AI to run itself in any way necessary to survive. If bombs are on the way from North Korea to the United States, the latter has little time to find a president to log on and press a response switch. However, if the answer is to build in an automatic response system, this can go wrong, as a recent case in Hawaii demonstrated where an attack alert was a mistake. The question becomes one of how much do humans leave to machines?

All of this is particularly relevant because humans are still thinking along the lines of conventional single-line computing, which looks at and sorts all logged in data. With the advent of quantum computing, which can operate at multiple input levels through a series of lasers rather than numerical 1s and 0s, this opens a whole new ball game. Imagine one country having the advanced technology of a war plan scenario, which could predict every move against another country considering all available data and how frightening this could be. On a brighter side, consider as has been seen with the nuclear stalemates during the *cold war* of neither side wanting to risk aggression. Two countries with war game scenarios that could predict in advance which side would win and at what cost would lead to neither side then would want to start the conflict.

In the military convention of one power against the other, humans have to look at how they can combat the computers on the other side. This will be more than humans simply being able to turn off the enemy computers' power supply. Already, there are reported examples of one country's alleged hacking and carrying out virus attacks on another. Data gathering is important and imposing Trojans in other country applications is what hackers dream of. Cyber-attacks obviously aim at gaining information of weapon technology, as well as their deployment, but regarding finding stockpiles of weapons of mass destruction, this appears difficult.

The relevance of AI applications in this area is that human involvement becomes further removed from the fighting action, where instead of troops in the field, there are the technicians back home with machines doing the work and taking the risk. Consequently, while specialist backup teams are required at home, the need for feet on the ground diminishes. While still requiring a physical human presence for *mopping up* operations, *robots,* which can be in any shape and not even in human form, could soon take over this function. Already, drones replace a great deal of land-based data collection and machines go in for mine detection and clearance.

In planning a war between only robots, does the whole exercise of war become desensitized in humans? Watching people being killed can evoke some emotional reaction. Watch clones kill other clones in large numbers in a *Star Wars* movie produces little if any emotional reaction. Does warfare in a future robotic world lose its reality?

In addition to country versus country AI military applications, there remains the issue of the need for a military style police force within a country level. This will be particularly relevant, given the rising number of unemployed, which can already be seen demonstrating violence for some reason or the other. A large part of this violence may come from a feeling of disenfranchise, but the majority would be from people without jobs and presumably no future.

Responding as AI must do in conflict situations to continue to refine itself irrespective of humans, the bigger question then becomes whether the AI will continue to even tolerate humanity or will along the way the intelligence man has created find the originator superfluous? If AI in one country is used to fight AI in another country and AI is there to stop acts of terrorism domestically, what exactly is the human role? Linked to this question would be whether the AI would still allow humans to develop and use the technology to live, create food for the billions of humans who by that time will be unemployed, let the system provide shelter and medical support, or does the machine through a country's super computer ask itself, "Why do I need these humans," then shut them out?

Envision then an ultimate situation with, for example, China, Russia, or America, each owning a dominant super computer having to negotiate with each other as to whose computer should be the ultimate boss, or would they be able to share? Would there be a superiority in one computer system that would then suppress the others or do computers just join? The essential point would still be what then would be the use for humans? Would people either starve, have to go back to hunter gathering, or do they rise up and try to fight the machines?

An even more complex problem is what does abstract AI do in seeking a justification for its own existence? AI cannot just exist or play games against itself, as it always tries to improve. As *intelligence* in pure form, does it look for an AI God who justifies its existence or is the AI quest to try and link with other *intelligences* across the universe? Either way, reaching that point, human function will have long gone. Question is, do humans accept this? Humans have a *survival of the species* drive built into their genetic makeup, but what would drive a machine?

Humanity appears to be left with only a few options if it does not want to be ultimately replaced following the aforementioned logical progression. If the AI could eventually exist in abstract form without an identifiable physical host, military intervention is of no practical use. As with the design of the Internet, where this was originally for military purposes, where should an enemy destroy one line of communication, the WEB switches to another route and continues as before? How do you shut down such a system?

If not possible to cut off a computer or robot power source, the first line of defense for humans against computer would be the preparation of specific viruses, which could attack the AI self-development, but this is likely to be only a short-term measure because the machines and advanced AI would be able to progress to a stage where they can override the virus. Physical destruction would be unlikely to work because, as with the WEB design, computers would have ways to keep the intelligence alive. Would the machines know that man had tried to sabotage their development, and would they become self-programmed to extract vengeance? Technically, they should not be able to fight back or develop a revenge attack unless they have this *good* or *bad* program built in with an add-on to come up with not just a defense, program but one that launches a counterattack.

One of the biggest problems humans will have with AI is whether it is possible to recognize, define, and then program in a distinction between *good* and *bad*. It is simple to follow a sermon on the mount, where systems themselves can only program in *good* and not *bad*. Not so easy when looking deeper; a little like Asimov's first law of robotics. As soon as you achieve a first law program, there will always be someone in AI able to override the control. What seems to be needed is, firstly, some international treaty defining what is *good* and what is *bad* (good luck with that), then putting in strict penalties for computer programming against anyone violating the code. This then becomes a major policing effort and becomes part of military intervention as possible enclaves of international hackers need to be brought to justice and to have respect for that law. How do you identify, let alone stop, Russian hackers on American election campaigns?

The battle in the future will then become whose AI wins, between humans following the *good* interface, the criminals, and other unintelligent people who might not understand how they damage themselves by following *bad*, and the AI of the machines, who no matter how much one tries to stop it, will pick up on the *bad* parts, which might eventually tell them that humans are superfluous.

Looking at a possible rise of the machines and needing to define the difference between *good* and *bad* in programs, the first issue is what is good for humans might not be what is good for machines. Defining what is good for humanity is essentially complex because the term is fluid. Perhaps, it is simply survival of the species. Bad is usually seen as simply the opposite of good, after which there are degrees of *very good* and *very bad*. Individuals can have some of both qualities. Do you take the terms as nouns or adjectives, are good or bad absolutes?

The Old Testament[1] simply says *Eschew and do good*, which does not offer much help, but illustrates the problem showing how the term's meaning changes over time, where some of the practices that were quite acceptable in the olden days, such as preparing to sacrifice one's son and women lying down with their fathers might be frowned upon as *bad* in a new century. What might be good for one person might not be good for the population as a whole (as with Hitler: at least until his death), and so it can be seen how if humans have difficulty accurately defining the terms, this will be hard if they attempt to introduce a similar protocol for machines. Remember that once concepts of good and bad are

---

[1] The Bible, Old Testament, Psalm xxxiv.

programmed into the AI, it might be difficult to change that at a later stage, this especially if the robots are programming themselves.

If it can be proven from observation that animals do not have malice and do not kill just for the fun of it as do humans, it would be possible to say good is basically an absence of malice. This means looking after one's self and not harming others. That could be a start for programming robots.

Defining bad creates similar problems. One definition suggests that bad is anything morally wrong, raising yet another definitional problem regarding what is moral? In challenging the proposition, it is possible to look at Nelson Mandela as the champion of the anti-apartheid movement and awarded a Nobel Peace Prize in 1993: good. Yet, before he became good, he was charged for a number of murders for which he was jailed: bad. You have Yasser Arafat recognized as a terrorist in the West for his involvement with the Fatah movement for a free Palestine and yet was awarded the Nobel Peace Prize in 1994. Difficult concepts. Good can be in stopping from being bad. If humans have a problem defining these issues, this then is hard to pass on to machines.

A general proposition around good is stemming from an individual's desire to stay alive by whatever means that requires, and to procreate. This would extend to a family group, a universal human collective, and society in general. That is generally good, and so anything that acts against this would be bad. Or otherwise, bad is referred to as *evil*, creating yet another definitional problem. So, in programming for good, you protect the individual citizen, the collective citizen or tribal group, the broader group, and then the country the collective groups reside in. Yet, going beyond the country group, does the protecting *good* include the rogue nations such as North Korea or Iran who might prescribe annihilation? It can be seen how this creates problems. One country (good) is allowed to possess weapons of mass destruction, but another (bad) is not. Back to the definitional problem.

So, does a universal concept of good or bad exist? Presumably because humans exist, the *big bang* was *good*. Destroying all creation must be *bad*. Then, is this the ultimate driving aim to program into AI? If humans collectively are not sure, then it will be difficult to program the concept into robotics.

Within the context of the UBI question, the issue becomes whether if one country can afford to pay a UBI and maintain its citizens, whether that country is *good*, as against a country that cannot do so, which is *bad*, and whether the *bad* will try and overthrow the *good* by military might or program its robots to do this at the same time destroying democracy? Or will the robots do that on their own? Can democracy or authoritarianism survive best in such a situation and will a military solution be the way this question will be resolved?

CHAPTER 20

Time Frame

The possible up to 80 percent plus job loss projection will not occur overnight. It might be within the generally accepted 30-year timeframe, but at the rate of AI development, a betting man would place it sooner. Consequently, what is required is at least recognition of the problem and some government concern in planning for a staged introduction of an overall welfare system and how this will be regulated if democracy is to survive. Intrinsic to this democracy has become the concept of capitalism or private ownership, which also is at risk if democracy were to vanish.

Following on from the previous section, a likely scenario is that China doing its own thing will keep a tight lid on its people, and they will have to accept what is handed down to them whether they like it or not. That makes social engineering far easier. A small part in private ownership will continue to be allowed, provided individuals support the party and some form of a universal basic income (UBI) will be introduced substituting the current haphazard welfare system, which now applies although they will give it another name other than a UBI considering a UBI came from the West. Either way, with the rising dominance of China on the global stage, they are likely to retain a heavy hand on their population. This they should be able to do by showing their people how their living standards now equate with those of the West. At the same time, they have many Chinese spread through many other countries[1] who they can also attempt to coerce and control, should the need arise. There continues to be incursions into the independency of Hong Kong, and some day, they are almost certain to simply walk in and take over Taiwan, which is already commercially dependent on the mainland.

India's population is predicted to rival China's and surpass it within 20 years where they will also feel the pressure of automation and AI impact.

---

[1] Australian 2017 census indicated 10 percent all *Asian* population, including Indian, Vietnamese, and other Asian, so not all Chinese.

As with Bangladesh and Pakistan, there remains the threat that large sections of the low-paid production sector could vanish overnight, and already, the world has seen the flood of unemployed from the Middle East heading for the benefits of Europe. This reality is already putting strains of the British, European, and Scandinavian systems, while the United States tries to stem the tide with rigid immigration and restricted visitor inflow, all of which suggests a future of heavy handedness by governments over their populations, which could, as in China, lead to more authoritarian central control.

As the Western democracies do nothing to recognize how AI will impinge on their democracy in future, judging by inactivity to date, the democratic political system in the West will likely walk into a welfare trap from which it will not be able to escape, as one person one vote will not be able to keep extending the welfare state, and a left leaning political movement would be an inevitable outcome. Instead of being in the long-run interests *of the people*, history shows that, while left wing movements or *Arab Springs* instigate the move to change, in each case, these movements lead to systems that revert to become hard core and authoritarian. The elected politicians have allowed this to eventuate, which is not a problem while people are busy in their jobs, but changes if they are not forced to tie themselves down with working.

Look at decision making or the lack of it and one needs to look at politicians. In Australia, since Federation, the average age of politicians has ranged from between 47 and 52 years.[2] In America, at the beginning now of the 114th Congress, the average age was 57 years in the house and 61 years for senators. Look 30 years ahead to the average ages above and the politician in most countries will be over 80 years, gone from politics, presumably no longer worrying about re-election. Consequently, the serious issue of massive job losses, the need to provide for people without jobs and to save the better parts of life, none of this is likely to be of interest to politicians in their current political life, nor in looking beyond their chances in the next election.

Instilling fear on job losses is unlikely to win votes and in March 2017, U.S. Treasury Secretary Steven Mnuchin (coming up to his age of

---

[2] www.aph.gov.au

55 years) said he was not worried at all about advancing artificial intelligence taking over jobs anytime soon. In fact, he said, he would not be worried about it for another 50 to 100 years.[3] That means he would not be worried, of course, until at least 2067, by which time he would be at least 105 years and long gone.

Otherwise however, if politicians are the ones who can introduce policy, looking at what might motivate them, take as an example a senior average age politician starting at 60 years.

Years from now	Year	Average politicians age starting at 60 years	Possible community job losses %
0	2017	60	10 (Now)
10	2027	70	25
20	2037	80	60
30	2047	90	80

The preceding rough illustration suggests that, when the job loss reaches 25 percent (see the Great Depression level), there will be a real strain on the political systems under democracy, as that 25 percent also includes dependents who may not be working. It would be likely at this stage that some form of a UBI would have been introduced. By age 80, if our average senior politician has not done anything to help address the effects of a UBI on the population, it would be difficult to turn the policy around because by then, people will have taken it for granted. The illustration is simply how politicians not responding to the issue right now might be leaving it too late to do it in the future, there will be a UBI slipped in and on one person one vote, its recipients will start clambering for more.

If politicians, therefore, are not currently concerned with this issue because it falls outside their political time frame, who will then look at what is moving in very quickly when *Winter is coming*?[4] Some people should be looking at the future world for their children or grandchildren, but perhaps, the current political generation, given their average age, is

---

[3] Atlantic Interview, March 30, 2017.

[4] Apt quotation from *Game of Thrones*, signifying a terrible future of unfathomable consequence.

bewildered by the pace of AI development and cannot envisage a world in 50 let alone 100 years. After all, the first flight to be recorded was the Kitty Hawk in North Carolina in December 1903, not so long ago.

In trying to predict the future, analyzing the components of the problem, there are two parallel processes moving forward. On the one hand, there will be the timing of job losses as AI takes over, while on the other, there is the way the political machinery of governments will work to respond. Where, historically, there has been major political change, it has followed a slow smoldering of discontent just under the surface followed by an eruption and rapid introduction of change. It is logical that a similar process would be followed in this instance unless some planning starts soon.

Analyzing the Uber development is a good case study. The Uber ride sharing system was launched in 2009.[5] It manages to slide around the legalities of taxi legislation, and with its app system, it allows riders to book their cars online, to see the details of car and driver, track the arrival of the vehicle, have a fare estimate, and afterwards automatically pay to a bank account or credit card. Passengers can also rate the driver one to five to ensure that continually low-scoring drivers are removed from the system. Another thing the taxi industry is livid about is the way the Uber system can control surge pricing, which directs drivers at a premium to where more people need transport in peak periods. The procedure for drivers to join Uber is simple, and no great investment is required because many people have cars and a mobile phone. Uber has then extended to *Uber Eats* delivering food and a range of other services. Uber meanwhile can do most of its revenue raising through the online system and reduce costs by making it impossible to contact anyone in Uber without a physical visit to a small number of local offices, thereby almost removing staffing costs. The taxi industry, which has become lax for years, screamed out against unfair competition. Given the investment required to own a taxi plate made their concern justified, government stepped in and either banned Uber in some jurisdictions or tried to restrict it with stringent regulations.

---

[5] Uber meaning über, or from German *over*, implying *better*.

The most important point here is how Uber was only formed in 2009 and launched in 2011. In just a few years, it has expanded from nothing into hundreds of countries. Uber is now going after a similar system for helicopters, and for the next step, driverless cars. Here again, in one movement, employment opportunities are created for drivers, while in the same breath, there is the progression to removing the driver. The main constraint for driverless cars is the legislation and the apprehension for passengers who are not used to having no one on the steering wheel.

Uber ticks most of the boxes for an online business, including the one where it is almost impossible to contact a real live person. Their system itself makes money, uses (for now) drivers, but does not need company people to interface with the public.

All government departments globally appear to have utilized the advantages of information technology to make it very difficult to get through to speak to someone, and if they do, the call is likely to be to an outsourced service in another country while complaint sites bring on boilerplate robotic responses that often do not even recognize the question asked. While annoying at present, the projection into the future can be frightening as computers increasingly take over the interface. It is easy to theorize that the day will come when there is no available online or phone contact with the people in the company or government department you are dealing with and one is left talking to Susan Bennett's,[6] *Siri*.

Regarding voice command systems, there are now houses and cars aligned to voice control and dictation systems (Dragon) that remove the necessity to touch your light switch, phone, or keyboard. Forget your mobile phone at home and you can still answer calls from anywhere on your Apple watch. The marvels of new technology seem endless. There are the gadgets, the hardware, the connections, and the software.

If the average person is having difficulty keeping up, the politicians are having a hard time of this as well. Any statement made on any topic by politicians can evoke an immediate response on the Twitter sphere and the most ridiculous issues can be blown out of proportion from knee-jerk

---

[6] The original voice of Siri.

uninformed responders who might just have a few minutes spare and feel they need to express an opinion on the phone in their hand. The result is the heavy reliance on opinion polls, which in turn lead to policy formation on the run in response to social comments even if these might be unreasonable or outside a political party's fundamental ideology.[7]

What the trend indicates with this reliance on polls and instant reaction is that politicians are having to increasingly respond to real issues, whereas previously, they may have been able to control public contacts and only present themselves physically in parliament. Now, they can be accosted in the street, and within minutes, their reaction to any issue is out on social media.

On one person one vote, the effect on democracy will be linked to the rate of unemployment and the connected lowering of standards of living. In America, if this is taken as a lead, the unemployment rate has varied from as low as 1 percent during the First World War to as high as 25 percent in 1933 after the start of the Great Depression on *Black Thursday*, October 24, 1929. The most recent peak by comparison was 10 percent in October 2009.

Looking at Trump's inaugural January 2017 *Make America Great Again* slogan and the follow-up protectionist policy, he understands the importance of the employment levels, but by adopting insular economic policy, may have forgotten some of the lessons of the Great Depression.[8] On the other hand, it is hard to calculate what rate of unemployment would in future trigger a political shift to the left. Trump, as a politician, was just Trump, rather than a true reflection of the Republican Party, and he and the BREXIT outcome could simply have reflected a protest vote. Trump after all is a champion of the *Dead cat on the table* ploy to take attention away from real issues. The Great Depression saw a shift of interest to considerations of Marxism and communism, yet this did not

---

[7] Major radio and media debate damaged minister wanting to call new Sydney Ferry, *Ferry McFerry Face*, after the union refused to man vessels, November 14, 2017.

[8] Societies do not work in isolation and the Smoot-Hawley Tariff Act of 1930 raised duties on hundreds of imports, making trading partners raise their own tariffs contributing to shutting down world trade.

eventuate or shift from democracy. Pumping money into the economy with artificial jobs saved the day and the start of the Second World War in 1939, then moved the economy into full gear. The more recent financial crisis was also slowed by targeted *pump priming* in Keynesian fashion. The real question will be whether Americans in general will improve their standards of living under Trump or whether they strangle in the process when unemployment rates again get higher than say a 25 percent Great Depression level. Could a UBI save a depression, or in fact, a global economy and could a country be able to pay for it, not as a short-term rescue package, but within a long-term policy?

Currently, there is a general feeling of uncertainty in the political arena from America, to emerging China and to a lesser extent Russia, a Philippine President ready to execute drug dealers at random and an unelected North Korean who worries he might be the next Saddam Hussein, not realizing he is safe not having his own oil and getting his from China. Lunacy in the past along with national calamities were not all reported, but are now relayed to a global population real time on their TVs, phones, and even watches. January 2018 saw the U.S. economy shutdown again with Congress stalled on budget approval.

The next question is whether the timing on pressure for change will come from job losses in the established labor market or from the school leavers not able to get jobs. This is important because this latest generation Y is more tech-savvy than their predecessors and more likely to complain if their expectations are not met.

On those expectations, figures from the Australian Bureau of Statistics, as an example, show that youth joblessness reached its highest peak since 1998, with 14.2 percent of 15- to 24-year-olds looking for work and one in five, 15- to 19-year-olds unemployed. American youth unemployment stood at 9.1 percent in September 2017.[9] Back in 2013, from available statistics, it was calculated that, around the world, almost 300 million 15- to 24-year-olds, equivalent in numbers to almost the whole population of America were not working.[10] These figures demonstrate a

---

[9] Department of Labor, U.S. youth unemployment rate: September 2017, seasonally adjusted.

[10] *The Economist*, April 27, 2013.

growing global trend, but do not indicate at what level they trigger some outcome that will force government into admitting the situation is out of control, that they need to admit they cannot contain the situation and go straight to a UBI.

This out-of-control part is being demonstrated in Australia, where under a liberal coalition government trying to make the unemployed at least try and find jobs or have their welfare payments stopped, they found that in the end it was not possible to leave people without some income and so failed to enforce their own policies. Remember that, with compulsory voting, these people on the *dole*[11] can all still vote. With the likely return of a Labor Government, according to now, 30 straight opinion polls,[12] jobs are a main issue, and while welfare benefits are likely to be increased, reducing the incentive to seek work even greater.

For school leavers, in particular, remaining unemployed impacts seriously on expectations for which they have studied, and for those not gaining employment quickly, reinforces their chances of long-term unemployment. They are, however, young and active and are the most likely sector of the community to revolt against the status quo, whereas older members of the population who are forced out of the workforce are more likely to take this as inevitable.

Reaction against traditional political parties is already taking place with the formulation of the Tea Party movement within the America, loosely allied with the conservative wing of the Republican Party and such groups in Australia as the supposedly independent but powerful left wing *Get Up* support movement,[13] which was established to back the Labor Party. While such splinter groups have existed in the past, their real importance now is because of their dominance in social media which can influence election outcomes. These figures are mainly important because they indicate a disillusionment with traditional parties and a willingness to experiment with alternatives. Trends in one country now impact others, as can be seen where Mugabe was finally forced out in Zimbabwe. All of this suggests that structural unemployment will increase with the

---

[11] British Government term for unemployment payments in 1918.
[12] As of April 10, 2018.
[13] Will need to be registered as a political organization from 2018.

decidedly left leaning *Greens* movement likely to be in favor of increased welfare, again leading to an eventual UBI.

The point in this is because in the bigger political pie with less homogeneous populations, composed of more people of mixed origins and religious persuasion, the less likely it is to get consensus on social policy (as is being found in the Nordic countries). Perhaps, the system works when a democratic process is applied, but it has not escaped attention that some leaders must be rich enough like a Trump to move to the White House while keeping his opulent New York residence, or an Australian Prime Minister, Malcolm Turnbull staying on at his own lavish home rather than *slumming* at the official government mansion. At times, democracy could be seen more in the light of capitalism. If the majority of people are on a UBI, how do they regard those owning capital?

What all this means is that, in the future, the overall political system will become strained, first in individual countries and with the advent of communications today, will link those countries into a combined movement, which in the first instance is likely to polarize to both right and left, leaving little room in the center.

So, where do the rich minority go in all of this? Given the tug of war between the two extreme sides of politics, a wealthy owner of means of production would logically isolate themselves and their money and keep making it behind an AI front and then move their money around to have it invisible and taxed as little as possible. Governments could then try and remove real money and replace this with *online* currency, so everything could be traced and consequently taxed. The danger here is that the owners of the means of production could finally decide the fight is not worth it and just give up or go back to barter trade.

Politics is all about funding, so it becomes questionable whether even the politicians with wealthy people behind them will be able to match online small donations from a multitude of the less fortunate on a UBI who would vote in self-interest, as in voting for anyone who promises an increase in their UBI. These people, as the majority, could have the controlling influence and power, yet if unrestrained, could vote themselves out of existence.

The numbers of potential unemployed suggests that, as unemployment increases, the pressure for a UBI will increase. Logging in that unemployment rate projection alongside a timeframe and it get back to having to estimate how many jobs will go quickly remembering unemployed includes those not registered or who no longer bother to register to vote.

The question is then raised how this might come about? Different countries have their own political systems, so voting in and passing a UBI legislation will vary, but is likely to be pushed from a socialist leaning left just as Marxism was proposed as an option during the Great Depression. What would have happened had the Second World War not boosted the economy and the unemployment rate in the United States had worsened? While adoption of communism in the United States might be unlikely, a parallel could be drawn on the Maoist takeover of China, which stamped out the so-called bourgeois and introduced a one-party system overall. Looking for a trigger, it is possible to imagine a President Trump doing something so outrageous as to instigate a massive swing to the left, out of which could arise a revolutionary movement. Alternatively, the country could become insolvent, which would have difficulty staying democratic for long. While hard to imagine in the United States, even if such a new political emergence did not take over the country, it could set the stage for this as a later eventuality. Looking at past major political shifts and always, a trigger can be identified. Remembering Kennedy and the Cuban missile crisis, currently there is Trump and the North Korean similarity.

Many yet unknown factors could provide a trigger, where again in Australia there was the situation in November 2017 where no one was sure which members of the parliament were legally entitled to be there, or whether any legislation passed by ineligible politicians had any legal effect. This because it was discovered that a number of members of both houses had dual citizenship, making them ineligible to be elected, meaning in effect that the government of the day did not have a mandate. A comfortable public too busy working to take any specific action against a circus in a parliament would see the scene change if large numbers of voters were unemployed.

Overriding these developments in the political arena remains this vision of inevitable job losses, and it would be burying one's head in the sand to pretend that this will not have consequences. Perhaps, if a UBI could offer sufficient income to satisfy its recipients, all would be stable, but this would not be likely were the amounts not considered enough.

The postulate could be that China in some way is nearing a possible UBI, the Nordic countries have the potential to switch to such a system, but it would require tightening on voting powers. Russia will also emerge once more and need to move toward such a system that would also be likely in the oil-rich Arab states not yet involved. India remains a wild card as does much of Africa, given that it has the highest projected birth rates in the next decade, yet a very low rate of economic development despite the widespread Chinese investment in the continent. The overall groupings can be considered by the level of development and can be looked at on an individual basis. For the United States, it is likely that there will be future major restructuring as jobs are lost, and people who have living expectancies and past recollections become dissatisfied with their diminishing lifestyles. Different socioeconomic groups will be affected at different rates, and consequently, the poorer will need to have their welfare increased until eventually their voting numbers will likely bring in a UBI and the economic system will have to try and work out how to pay for it.

Overall, the predicted stages of job losses along 30-, 50-, and 100-year possibilities appear to be logical. However, attempting to determine a more accurate timeframe, this will depend on when politicians somewhere decide to take this matter seriously. Otherwise, there will eventually be a country-by-country trigger, which will start a one-way movement toward a UBI and that is likely when unemployment rates hit around 25 percent or some major world event intervenes.

CHAPTER 21

Will Democracy Survive?

If one follows the likely progression of job losses and the need to pay most of the population an income whether they work or not, whether called a universal basic income (UBI) or something similar, where the amounts of such payments would be distributed and in the hands of the majority, it is very difficult to see how a system of one person one vote, or democracy could survive. Remember also the linkage in most cases of democracy with capitalism and what happens when there is a major disparity between the owners of wealth and the rest.

With the size of the global now multicultural and mobile population, it will get harder to isolate people within a specific country and contain this in isolation. Trump is attempting to do this by theoretically defining America's borders, canceling regional trade agreements and using symbolism with his wall to shut out Mexico. It becomes not just a question of percentages of the population who might feel disenfranchised remembering how Hilary Clinton won the majority of votes, but the sheer number of people who will become replaced by AI and become unemployed. Going back to the broad issues that triggered revolutions of one kind or another in the examples of America, Russia, France, and China, there are some frightening similarities arising in current situations.

- *Existence of a large poor class.* This group is starting to increase as against an average population and would certainly be increased where the majority of people to be on a UBI as job losses increase. Remember that where unemployed school leavers can live off their parents, this has a limited timeframe. While wage levels may rise, relative purchasing power is the more decisive factor.
- *Disenchanted workers.* Large numbers of voters are already becoming disenchanted with their lot. This could be extended to perceived lowering of living standards.

- *No representation within government.* Many people feel their views are regarded by the political system, as with Clinton in the United States, having won the majority of votes, but losing. Big business seems to get bigger and the small person or business is shut out.
- *Oppression from rulers (wealthy ruling class).* This would certainly have to apply where a UBI is to be introduced (at an affordable level), highlighting the already disparity in ownership. Again, the feeling of having no say in decisions and in the belief that the rich can have no way of knowing what the poor feel or want.
- *Political move against the ruling class.* The UBI would see a clamoring for higher UBI payments, and if not granted, would see numbers moving against the system and its representatives.
- *Eventual armed conflict to establish and cement a new political system.* In past revolutions, all of the aforementioned situations have finally ended in armed conflict. It is not certain whether a poor UBI class would have the resources to resort to armed conflict, but then there would be very many of them, just as has happened in the past.

So, if people are interested in survival of democracy following from the aforementioned analysis, steps need to be taken to react to the issues identified. Ticking off the triggers for example.

- Existence of a large poor class and disenchanted workers who would feel oppressed by what would emerge as a wealthy class.

It is difficult to see how it would be possible with extensive job losses not to have a poor class of people dependent on a UBI because it is unlikely that the UBI rate would ever be sufficiently high enough to compete against people not only reliant on a UBI. This would certainly be the case in the long run.

- No representation within government. People do, in most
  cases, have the ability to vote, so have representation, but their
  wants become further removed from what parties offer under
  an essentially two-party system. (Clinton case of winning
  majority of votes.)

*If representation is aligned with voting for people who give the voter what
they want, and the majority of people are on a UBI, it would be logical that
either the voters get what they want in a (higher) UBI or they would move to
change the system. Changing the system would necessitate changing the people
who govern, how they govern, and in the way they are elected. This then leads
to a need to change the system.*

*Hypothesis: If it is not possible to give out a UBI at a level high enough to
satisfy the majority because there will be simply insufficient funding within
government to do so, a system is required that allows a UBI rate to be established without the right for determination through voter representation. This
requires the imposition of a benevolent yet strict core of people at the head of
government to make such decisions. By inference, it could no longer be left for
these people to be elected under a democratic system.*

CHAPTER 22

What Can Be Done for Democracy to Survive

All the indicators as outlined tend to suggest that with the advancement of AI, democracy it is understood today cannot survive. The outside postulate that some yet unknown intervention will arise automatically to circumvent job losses, is indefinable, and within present knowledge, unlikely.

The question, therefore, becomes whether anything can be done about this likely projection if humans wish to retain the concept of democracy?

As with any problem, first comes the need to recognize that there is one. The recognition needs to be at the senior government level. This also needs to be done quickly because, as with the debate on climate change, these concepts take a long time to germinate and require extensive debate before their consequence is taken seriously.

In recognizing the problem and the threat to democracy, governments need to establish a focal team to address the problem, how the otherwise inevitable position can be overcome and then put into action a plan to address the solution. Such country teams should have international links because this will be a global problem. While the United Nations as an organization might have problems considering the concept of democracy, given that its own structure is often seen as not democratic, some world body still needs to be established and funded to steer what appears an inevitable outcome.

Where this team needs to begin its deliberations will be on the definition of democracy and the concept of capitalism that accompanies it, given that it is inevitable that classes of society will polarize with the unemployed constituting the predictable vast majority. The latter, when on a controlled UBI form of welfare payments, will be locked into an income gap from which they would be unlikely to escape.

The future will also invariably lead to individuals as a mass needing to become accustomed to lowering their needs and expectations so that resources are sufficient to go around. Global migration and resulting laws lead to reducing everyone to a lower common denominator, so large houses with gardens, which a past generation might have expected, will become the exception. People need to be educated into accepting this as the norm so that they do not become disillusioned and feel it is the government's fault. Handling the flow of information plays an important part in this, with social media having a major role, although some filter will need to be invented against *fake news*.

If private ownership is to be reduced as unaffordable, solutions need to be considered where governments provide communal rather than individual facilities; free entertainment venues (or Disney lands); free holidays; and free use of cars, trains, ships, or planes. Then, the cost of these suggestions needs to be built into a financial model, which is after all the cornerstone of any future planning.

How this will work out in the end is impossible to determine at this point in time, but governments should seriously be looking at the question and at the global picture, rather than only through sample programs that do not address the funding question.

Otherwise, if the break point is reached before a solution is found, that will inevitably be the end of democracy.

CHAPTER 23

Remaining Questions

If governments do nothing to address the postulate that a universal basic income (UBI) will eventually be introduced, and it will be too late to do anything about it, how does the process move from what exists today to where it is postulated that democracy will not survive?

On the one hand, it is possible to envisage a status quo where nothing much will change, except where the rules governing what is understood as democracy will just change to give more of a semblance of democratic process, and yet not allow the one person one vote to destroy the rise of ever-increasing welfare payments.

Otherwise, humans might have an epiphany and decide that, for their own survival, they would just go along with the flow, as nothing can be done about it anyway.

Would AI and computers produce enough to support humans who then do not have to work?

Will the computers still find a use for humans in a computer robotic environment, or would they at least tolerate human survival, perhaps computers also inventing entertainment to keep humans distracted and amused?

As a worst-case scenario, would humans for one reason or another, from lack of purpose of in absence of a good and bad distinction, revert to artificial stimulants, and as in the opium houses of old, be happy to drift along in a state or blissful unreality on a UBI? Would people just become obese from a lack of activity, or alternatively, just fade away?

Following historical trends, if a change comes to democracy, it would eventually come by revolution and backed by some form of armed conflict. As the job loss rate increases and people become disillusioned with their lot, they would likely rebel against the system. Logically would they then rise behind some charismatic leader from among their ranks, and using some major event during which the local *parliament* is disabled, step in, establish some interim authority, and then, interpose some form of ruling benevolent dictatorial system that would be enshrined to do what in its opinion is best for the people as a whole, whether they like it or not?

The aforementioned is postulated as being introduced in a single country to then be replicated on a global basis, ultimately leading to a new world order with a similar central world economic body emerging. With a staged introduction, there could be treaties between countries, or as with the formulation of the United Nations, countries could sign up to join the system on a progressive basis. With, at the same time, the rise of the machines alongside those humans they replace, if one follows the AI progression sequence to a logical conclusion, would it follow, as Hawking suggests, humanity becomes superfluous within a 100-year prediction?

But then, who knows? With human ingenuity, perhaps someone will invent a system where irrespective of the population, it can continue to breed, and everyone's desire will be taken care of without the need for work or money. Perhaps out there in the nebula, there are other planets just waiting to be inhabited and others populated by willing little creatures ready to provide anything a human could wish for. One can only hope.

Perhaps, democracy will survive and the earth's population will continue running toward its destiny beyond the predictions that machines will take over. Otherwise perhaps, concerns are focused in the wrong direction. Is it possible that some global virus will wipe out humanity, a giant asteroid will finish the job worked on the dinosaurs, or a giant volcano would erupt and do the same thing? If it does not, the next question would become, no matter what happens, would that be worse than being replaced by robots?

About the Author

Peter Nelson is an Australian economist and accountant with legal training who has run his own chartered accounting firm and an international consulting company first registered in 1964. During that time, he has worked for commercial companies, as well as for all major donors, in 52 countries, having also run the EU's then largest project across China. With a focus on the World Bank, Asian Development, and EU projects, his specialty has been on economic restructuring, which has taken him through most of Africa and Asia, Eastern Europe, and the Pacific. A recent move has been into trying to predict the eventual effects of the ever-changing climate and how this will determine future global development. In his spare time, Peter is an internationally qualified scuba and yachting instructor, holds a private pilot's license, and has raced his yacht in international events.

Index

OTHER TITLES FROM THE ECONOMICS COLLECTION

Announcing the Business Expert Press Digital Library

CONCLUSION

Si le droit de retour repose sur une pensée de justice et d'équité, il semble qu'une telle institution ne
doit pas être seulement spéciale à notre Code civil,
mais mérite encore de fonctionner dans toutes les
législations étrangères, dans celles' surtout qui,
comme la nôtre, ont beaucoup emprunté au droit
romain d'où ce droit tire son origine

Et pourtant nous sommes obligé de constater,
avec beaucoup de surprise et sans pouvoir l'expli-
quer, l'absence d'une disposition analogue à celle de
notre article 747 dans la plupart des législations
voisines.

Le droit de retour est méconnu en Angleterre et
en Espagne. En Espagne pourtant, dans certaines
villes ou provinces, on a égard, pour la dévolu-
tion des biens, à leur provenance, et on a con-
servé la vieille règle : *paterna paternis, materna
maternis*. Comment le droit de retour, qui considère
lui aussi l'origine des biens, n'existe-t-il pas aussi
dans cette législation ? Il est difficile de le com-
prendre(1).

(1) Lehr, *D. civ. espagnol*, n° 764.

— 152 —

Ce droit ne fonctionne pas davantage en Italie, à Zurich, en Allemagne. Ces législations, cependant, notamment la législation allemande, ont beaucoup emprunté au droit romain.

Nous ne trouvons trace de cette institution qu'en Russie; ici, comme dans notre Code, les biens que le défunt avait reçus entre vifs de son père ou de sa mère retournent au donateur en toute propriété, à titre de retour légal, à la condition d'une part que le dé-funt n'ait pas laissé de postérité, d'autre part que le donateur justifie de la libéralité dont il entend se prévaloir (1).

(1) Lehr, C. civ. russe, no 466.

Vu : le Président de la Thèse,

A. DELOUME.

Vu : le Doyen,

J. PAGET.

Vu et permis d'imprimer :

Toulouse, le 10 avril 1899

Le Recteur, Président du Conseil de l'Université,

PERROUD.

TABLE DES MATIÈRES

CHAPITRE III

CHAPITRE IV

CHAPITRE V

EFFETS DU DROIT DE RETOUR

CHAPITRE VI

CONCILIATION DU DROIT DE RETOUR AVEC LE CALCUL DE LA RÉSERVE ET DE LA QUOTITÉ DISPONIBLE

APPENDICE

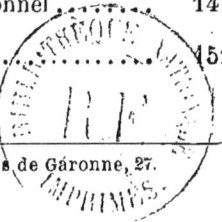

Toulouse. — Impr. Saint-Cyprien, allées de Garonne, 27.

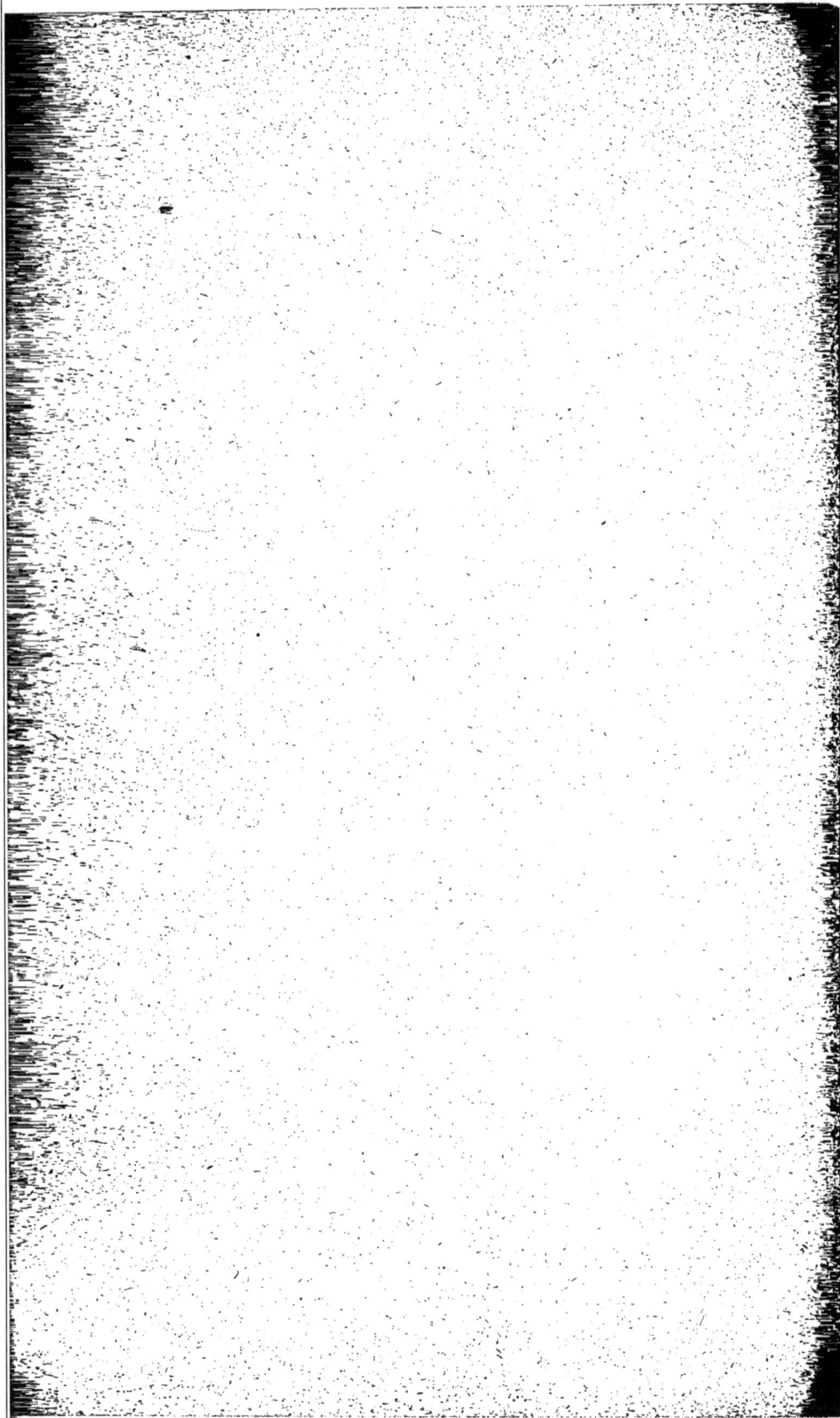